AGENDA

New Generation Poets

AGENDA

CONTENTS

ESSAYS

POEMS

REVIEWS

TRANSLATIONS/VERSIONS

NOTES FOR BROADSHEET POETS

BIOGRAPHIES

Front cover painting: Lilltangen (Little Seaweed Harbour).
Oil on wood.
Catherine McIntosh received her MAFA in
painting from Edinburgh College of Art. She
currently lives, paints and works in Nelson,
a small mountain town in British Columbia,
Canada.

Introduction

Agenda has, for thirteen years now, been especially encouraging the work of young poets, many of whom had their very first published poems highlighted in *Agenda*'s pages, and in *Agenda*'s online Broadsheets for young poets and young artists. It is most encouraging to see, therefore, that a considerable number of these poets have, since then, gone on to have their work published in pamphlets and collections, and even to become quite established.

This New Generation Poets' double issue is a testament to the energy and fresh talent in these Broadsheet poets and other poets today. Some of these original Broadsheet poets have gone on to become academics, usually in the field that we are debating here: Creative Writing.

'Can you teach Creative Writing, especially Poetry?' was put to the distinguished essayists and tutors included in this issue and, as you can see when you read on, this question throws up many different responses, complexities and questions both positive and negative, and throws light on the fact that Poetry is a real industry nowadays.

Peter McDonald, in the Sheila Smyth Memorial Lecture, 'The Learning of Poetry', that he delivered in the Methodist College, Belfast on the 28th September, 2012 (subsequently published in *Yellow Nib*), succinctly introduced his subject by asking 'Are poets born, or made?' or can they be both 'born *and* made'? 'There is the idea that a poet is someone profoundly special – differently attuned to the world, and to language – who is possessed by nature of certain gifts: it is this character who cannot be manufactured, or otherwise artificially brought into being. At the other end of the spectrum, we have the idea of a poet as somebody who is the product of a whole cultural enterprise, fashioned out of life and society, literary tradition, knowledge, and careful training.' And this is surely, as you can detect in the ensuing pages, where the debate lies.

As Peter McDonald suggests, 'One way of thinking about the rise in Creative Writing is as the triumph of manufacture over that rarer, and much harder to define thing, inborn poetic talent'. There is no doubt that, in any country or society, there is only a given number of genuinely gifted poets. Some work on in isolation, teaching themselves by reading poetry.

Geoffrey Hill (in 'Strongholds of the Imagination,' interviewed by Alexandra Bell, Rebecca Rosen, and Edmund White, (*The Oxonian Review*, Issue 9.4, 18 May 2009) endorses this: 'I believe that poets should be self-taught, based on an intensive programme of preferably serendipitous reading'. He is quite sceptical about Creative Writing degrees, though he exempts the Oxford Chair of Poetry and the Christopher Tower Chair at

Christ Church; 'these are currently in very good hands and the emphasis on traditional teaching methods is probably firm'. There is no doubt that other would-be poets enrol on Creative Writing degrees or workshops, sometimes in the mistaken belief that a qualification here will automatically turn them into real live 'poets' who can live by their gift when, Geoffrey Hill would argue, they are merely being provided with 'a kind of therapy'.

Peter McDonald continues in a similar vein: 'They are much more likely to be learning how to write in a style of acceptable mediocrity, in line with the prevailing styles of "successful" poetry. Self-esteem may be boosted – though it may be lowered, too – in this process; and every now and again, published poems (or more) may even result; but that the art of poetry is being served in any way by this commercial form of art-therapy seems to me deeply implausible. And we should not forget that commercialism here is not incidental, but central: if workshops did not pay, they would not happen.'

Craft can of course be taught, and this is often magnificently done, and gives the students an extra articulacy in communication necessary for general life-skills, but is that 'divine spark' something that can be elicited by a tutor?

There is a story about Rimbaud, age fifteen, being entered for a national sonnet-writing competition at school. He was the only entrant from Charleroi and the invigilator had noticed after two and a half hours of the three hour exam that Rimbaud had not put pen to paper. He asked him if anything was wrong. He replied 'I'm starving. Go and get me a croissant!' Needless to say he came first in the whole of France with his poem, following all the classical rules of form and structure. University would most likely have ruined him! It does happen the odd time that a student with a very strong, original gift gets their own distinctive voice ironed out of them by exercises with 'targets' and 'assessment objectives' on a Creative Writing course. I am thinking of a young friend who had extraordinarily gifted poems in *Agenda* at the age of sixteen. She sent me lifeless, bland poems while at a very reputable university studying Creative Writing, came out with a first class degree, but then declared she did not think she could ever write a poem again. Luckily, after seven years, she has at last rediscovered her lost voice and come out with a poem.

Perhaps, I would moot, for a potential poet, to gain a degree in something other than Creative Writing or even in Literature – like Anthropology, History, Medicine or whatever – would give greater ground for inspiration. Otherwise the student is a tabula rasa: what is there to write about with, usually, very limited life-knowledge? Also, how objective can examiners be in evaluating Creative Writing tasks? Peter McDonald endorses this: 'For what "creative writing" is not – and never can be – is an academic discipline;

it does not have access to the depth of critical argument, scholarship, philology, and literary history that have traditionally fed into the discipline of English literature.' He adds, 'You cannot learn to be a poet, you can learn poetry, as well as learning about it, and the intellectual and cultural virtues of this are very considerable.'

The American Pushcart Prize-winning poet, Doug Anderson, goes further, blaming Creative Writing degrees for small audiences at poetry readings: 'To what do we owe poetry's small audience? Jack Gilbert said the audience has always been small, that not everybody can get poetry. I don't believe it. I think that poetry, particularly academic poetry – that is poetry that comes from MFA program students and faculty – is to some degree responsible for its small audience. I was at a large reading at AWP in Austin and remember the poets, reading principally to other poets and friends, seemed to be laughing at in-jokes. This is the elephant in our poet's living room: how do we reach a larger audience without compromising quality?'

'In-jokes'– how often these prevail, what Geoffrey Hill calls 'the easy chuckle' aimed at by many poets on the circuit.

To end on a mainly positive note, however, it is worth listening again to Peter McDonald: 'It needs hard work and time; that as well as feeling oneself to be a poet, there is the long business of learning how to write true poetry, which may take a lifetime.' A lifetime indeed, like the many years, up to twenty or more, spent by the ancient Celtic Bardic schools, which proved that the elongated kind of study by the singers and poets (themselves 'carpenters of song') in the craft of Poetry was worthwhile, maybe because most of them were *fílí* or seers anyway, second in rank only to the King. Never mind that they would, today perhaps, be labelled elitist since they were chosen from amongst the ruling aristocracy, part of the learned class of priests, teachers and judges known as 'Druids'.

Ted Hughes, introducing a poetry reading in 1988, spoke of these ancient Bardic schools for poets as 'the first colleges in the British Isles, for centuries the only colleges' for poets expected to carry on their backs 'the whole culture of the people'. The Arvon Foundation, set up by Ted Hughes, in Lumb Bank and Sheepwash is a worthy Foundation, offering week-long residential courses not only in poetry, with experienced, published tutors, but also in fiction, screen writing, drama etc. Then, of course, there are the genuinely well-deserved universally prestigious poetry prizes such as the Griffin Poetry Prize (won, recently by *Agenda* poets Michael Longley and Éilean Ní Chuillenáin), the T S Eliot Poetry prize (won very recently by Sarah Howe interviewed in this issue, and, last year, by David Harsent, long associated with *Agenda*), the Forward Poetry Prizes, and the National Poetry Competition.

St John Perse, it must be remembered, said poets, who are a 'vital force', write 'pour mieux vivre et plus loin' ('to live better and further') and, 'it is through the grace of poetry that the divine spark lives in the human flint'. It is this 'divine spark' that *Agenda* seeks in every poet.

Doug Anderson, a horse devotee like myself, would like the analogy with the Sport of Kings: good hands (when riding a horse), like poets, are born, not made! Indeed, they were often seen as a fairy gift.

Appreciators and readers of poetry must not be left out here, and even if as Yeats writes in 'Galway Races':

> We too had good attendance once,
> Hearers and hearteners of the work

it is important to

> Sing on: somewhere at some new moon
> We'll learn that sleeping is not death,
> Hearing the whole earth change its tune...
> Its flesh being wild and it again
> Crying aloud...

to produce 'hearteners', as I am sure are all of you who read *Agenda*!

To give Yeats the last word: it is worth remembering for those who perhaps are not 'born poets' that, had his love for Maud Gonne been requited, even the 'born poet' Yeats would 'have thrown poor words away/ And been content to live'.

Patricia McCarthy

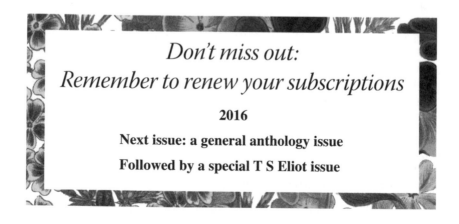

Don't miss out:
Remember to renew your subscriptions

2016

Next issue: a general anthology issue

Followed by a special T S Eliot issue

Anna Lewis

The First Crusade

Bluebell woods, chalk downs are distant now:
an arm of water separates the things
themselves from memory,

and so with each mile into Normandy
the chalk glows brighter, bluebells thicken.
Through the green shade of Bavaria,

above the pummelled path of the Danube,
across the Dardanelles where Europe
crumbles into sun and dusty latitudes;

south, east, towards the dome:
the stud, the bolt, the rivet at the core.
As they near the city walls

each must close his eyes and think again:
of chalk white as a christening-gown,
the downland houses overrun with flowers.

Sunday or No

Catania

After all, it is December,
the hillsides rough with smoke.
At night in skinny jeans,
black knee-high boots and leather coats,

sopranos practise in the church;
angels beat wooden wings,
the star rises and sinks along its wire.
It is the brink of winter,

it is almost time to rest. Sunday or no,
today in high plots and allotments
men are taking in the crops,
green armfuls pressed to bony chests;

at noon they prop their spades and forks
against the wall, carry out chairs,
and open wine. The sun hangs just
above their heads, their liver spots.

The Hum

The child is there beneath the sand,
is tucked with forehead dropped to knee
beneath the sand floor of the cave,
the cool, insistent hands
of amulets holding it down.

The parents walk above its face,
its curving back, its hips.
They sleep, grind corn
and skin the kill; make new children,
who cry and crawl and dash their fists

against the ground; who, on their sides
around the grey remains of fire,
lie silent as hyenas bark,
as aurochs low. The night is unlit,
and the stream runs through the woods

more loudly than it does by day.
The children push their fingers
in between their gums,
and suck: the salt,
the warm, the hum of blood.

The High Path

On a fine, shallow day – a day of larks,
of aeroplane trails vivid as the cropmarks
that surrender ancient plots and fields –

the path across the moor is clear and dry,
and as the hills rise, so the path
lifts into unrestricted light.

But here, and here, along its side:
waymarks three thousand years old.
Each nods silently toward the next.

The reeds and bog grass quickly dim,
the river's silver in an instant slims,
and when the cloud descends

there is no white-dashed road below,
no hotels muscled to the estuary wall;
there never have been.

Whoever dug the earth out
to receive these stones, whoever tipped
and fixed them in position,

knew the ease with which
we become lost – and not in the sense
of metaphor, not in the sense

of spirit, mind or heart, but here:
within the fog, upon the moor,
along the same high path.

Richie McCaffery

Corners

One thing my father told me
in appreciating old buildings
was that once upon a time
architects celebrated corners.

Where streets traded names
and the wind turned political,
pro or anti in your face –
the prettiest houses stood.

He said if he could afford
to choose, he'd have lived
on the corners of many streets
in towns unfallen from grace.

He taught me not to fear
changes of direction, but pause
in passing and consider
an edifice of past and future.

Today I'm turning a corner,
its house has curved windows,
the stone is solid and rounded
and quite something to behold.

Window tax

You don't believe me when I say
there was once a window tax –
our view bought or bricked up.

Even now, centuries on, walking
through Elie, you see mocked up
sashes of paint on stone,

yet to be undone and glazed
as if the owners
are afraid they'll be fined,

for looking out and longing
more clearly than ever,
for some place else.

A study of bannisters

Our first house had an old
sweeping mahogany bannister,
when I was young and because
I was young, I thought
it was only for sliding down.

My grandparents' house
had a boxed-in staircase
and nothing to hold onto,
but you could shout down
for sweets, sounding like a god.

They had a new bannister fitted
and began to lean heavily
on their breathless ascents.
It was like I'd been born
into an old world, just as they

began to die in something new.
I will always be glad our lives
met in this manner on the stairs
even if they said such crossing
was considered to be bad luck.

Abegail Morley

Last words

That night, two hours after, in a narrow bed
in a cheap hotel, time reverses like egrets

retreating ungainly into egg's seamless
backstitching. Unhealed wounds repair

under a dim 40 Watt bulb, skin clings to skin
until scars flicker like splinters in shell.

I take your words, crack each one, release
yolk from white, hide them till my pockets

burst with sunbeams or fat yellow buttons
purled to fabric. I know you want them back,

to somehow unhatch them, catch each one,
hold them captive. But I shackle them

to my wrists, don't even flinch as I do it, broil
each of them with the heat of my hands.

The Just dead

Once she told me dead people paint our faces
on walls like we're shadows of ourselves.
They don't have walls like us; both they
and their bodies roam freely. Time is smooth,
hums like a fridge in a still kitchen.
I think of myself as their shadow-being, imagine
how they spread me, joyride curves of cheekbones
in the howling dark, prise open my portrait
till they discover memories of themselves
thumping like lorries over Battersea Bridge.
They find my imaginings in the blink of my eye,
pluck each lash – *she loves me, she loves me not,*
harbour each thought in their pursed palms.
Sometimes I think they devote their lives to me
and I exist in their memories, not mine.
Sometimes I think things I shouldn't write down –
but I do. I know they wear my skin like an
ornamental robe, flash me around at parties.
A part of me wishes I was there, if only to serve
the drinks. I carry the burden of the dead.
In my head they're carved black lines, lightning
struck stumps, torn hair yanked out in fistfuls.
Some nights I can see their vanishing points,
know they scrape around my house,
pause and unpause themselves like shadows.

Jessica Traynor

Céide Fields

First things caught
in the light of memory –
the tiger-striped melamine table,

my granddad's jumper,
with its Blockbuster pattern,
my narrow granny

washing up by the sink.
Outside this kitchen
the world dissolves

in darkness,
but here my granny's paused,
dishcloth in hand,

recalling a trip
to the Céide Fields,
with peat-pickled relics

tanned by millennia
to the colour of still pools
or faded bloodstains,

and shadow-villages
pushing up through blanket bog
like secrets wanting to be told.

I'm a child in love with the past,
and these stories map
a route beyond the real –

my granny saying
they were just like us
as somewhere outside time

a girl holds out her hand to me,
but then my granddad's lip
is trembling, he's saying

over and over, *but,*
the little children,
but, the little children...

My granny's mouth hardens.
When he leaves the room
and I ask her why he cried,

she starts to dry the dishes,
stares at the space
above my head

as if she's found a portal
to the passage I had found
and wants to wall it up.

Note:
The Céide Fields, situated in Co. Mayo, are the world's most extensive Stone Age
monument.

Eels

I grew up in a swarm
of electric eels
who'd twist in their skirts,
writhing to escape.

Sometimes static
would shimmer through
their skin; and if
you caught their eye

you'd see the spark
that lived there.
Each of them
married a shadow

who acted the maggot,
always in search
of a body, and my eels
cried crackling tears,

their voltage soaring,
until the time came
when they'd pin you
with a stare,

pull you close,
and fry the heart
in your chest.

Tom Thumb's Arch

When Mr Patel gives me the keys,
I find it difficult to disperse
the ecologies of silence that gather
around the abandoned Raki bottles,

that flow from one source –
the missing Russian tenant's wardrobe,
still stuffed with clothes: the dresses
of a woman taller than me.

In my dream that night I put on
her sequined blue skirt, slit to the thigh,
her three furred hats and her mac;
salvage from the floor one false lash,

secrets caught in its spider legs.
I fix it to my forehead, walk
the Roman Road, through chained-up stalls,
past Bow Church and its silent bells

to stand under Tom Thumb's Arch,
touch its ceiling with cold fingers –
a giant in a glove-close sky,
drowning in a dead woman's clothes.

Jacob Eoin Agee

Land Orcas

Slugs
on the move at dusk,
beached
on the dunes above
Magheraroarty Strand.

Crash and fall
of wave on wave,
and they push on,
mollusc along.

Slime lines on dank sand
glistening like
sugary cookies
in the grainy half-night light.

Surf and drizzle,
salt in sand,
our stroll over
mussel-like mini-whales

and frosty slug-trails'
crystal-blazing
on the dune shoulder's
darkling surface.

Gecko

Hounds' howl and the crickets' diminuendo.
But when a gecko's there he stays, still as a star.
Edging an inch an hour towards his roosting moth.
His body's an unmoving pulse.
His eyes freaky, one-minded pods.
He's got a gooseberry hue, or is
Coarse and spotted black-on-evergreen,
Or of an almost-lucent pale.
Newt of dry lands, always talisman.

He tholes the still wait.
On a moony harmattan
Of lit, cooling limestone.

Look down in the kitchen at night, and one might be
A quick phantom across the sališ.
Sometimes at bedtime, one's small and sudden
On the wall, in an obscure place to look at,
But ineluctable once seen.
A little ghost, frozen and expressionless
Up on lit-white limestone, staring.
A watcher-over, of the room once shared.

Note:
sališ: traditional Dalmatian flagstones (Croatian).

Bóin Dé

Little cow of God –

As if from Lilliput, you land on my knee—
Polka-dotted, tortoise-shaped—
Where I read *Tom Sawyer* one blue afternoon
On the chair beneath the walnut tree.

You belong to life in the undergrowth,
Which I was accustomed to brush through, flush out,
Cup and bottle till a collection
Built up on my bed, an exhibition

The two of us would show to all and sundry.
Scarabs green as Mljet, crickets with their red capes
And bulging eyes, dappled spiders
Magnified in the refracted light.

You were too small, though, ladybird –
For whom the spider's web spells death.
And I think how you flew from the field where she stood,
Blond and delicate, those blue afternoons;

Where her almond tree now comes of age
Like the life of the loss itself,
Small and beautiful, still as a Buddha.
Now you fly away to the ground whence you came,

Where the hay will regrow, where
The spider's web will spell death again.

Note
Bóin Dé (Irish): ladybird (literally, 'little cow of God').

Andrew McMillan

before mass

I have already laid it out in front
of me   the choreography of bells
and silence   how I will walk behind you
into the palace of light   and insist
we sit at the back   where the empty
mouths of the collection plates will be shocked
as we are to have fetched up here   Belleek
on a Sunday   the Father ascending
to his lectern   young boys stood patient
at the edges   and the sermon will be 'love'
or rather proper love   that which is not
an abomination   and my forehead
will be wet with sweat   and I'll try to picture
Jesus in your dining room   in the golden
frame   looking like a pale man others have
adorned   and suddenly I'll be standing
and my feet will be so small in the vast house
and you'll follow   all the way to the beach
where the waves are turning over like tables
and I'll let my anger sink down
to the bottom of my soles   and take your palm
and press the wet pink flesh of it to mine

after mass

there is talk of Heaven over the buffet
of whether I can expect to go there
christened as I am but now an atheist
and wondering what it might look like

would it be this?   a family sat around
in love and laughing   I cannot hope
to enter that which I cannot conceive of
all I can call into comprehension

is some small personal morsel   that feeling
after sex   emptiness   contentment   hazed
with loss   and just laying there   breath urgent
in the body   the white sheet bearing up
our newly separate selves

Ailie MacDonald

White, Black, Red River

After reading Mungo Park's Travels in the Interior of Africa

Sweet Senegal, aye
nine long hours we rode
steep in the thrall of those soft-battered shores –
the bull-river of a swell behind us,
rolling on and on
over the rough burr-hole of the ocean.

The sea here grows to a verdant hill
its peaked craw rattled by the spindrift
and soon-forgotten breaths of shingle:
an inverse mark of rock
as it breaks upon the sky
like the calls of a black-tongued mother ewe.

We watch for the land to part its red mantled fins
with our libations tipped, ready
in makeshift spearhead cups –
no mother to bring us milk
but the heat of the brass-hot sky
and the lines of sediment sunk to mud.

We, like babbling infants
swarm to watch it from over the gunwales,
the broad-backed meniscus of the ocean
long and low under the paunch of the sky,
A vast-bodied fish, spun belly-up
to bare swollen gut to the current of the red river.

Like a freed slave your voice gurgled down to the sea,
to the brackish water,
and the pock-marked stone.

Words,
bold and glutinous beings.
Lips,
wet with their first remorseful utterance.

Aye, and though you turned your back on that loveliness
it is not gone
but harries on:
the cold rag of a crow,
clutching the branch.

James Simpson

Tiger Head Sonnets

vii

My grandfather lies in shadows;
lies with a woman
whose body is that of a tiger.
The room is silent;
and shadows like stripes
cast across her back.

How can he return home
across moors with the sea fretting;
back to smoke-stained tenements,
to a bound suspect God
and the sleeting rain?

Blind Tiger, is it true of angels
that they fail to see through
the unremitting dark?

viii

Young women in saris
are singing carols;
neon strobes the bedroom ceiling,
the city's traffic is perpetual.

Let us enter the forest at night,
let us go to the place
where they set snares.

In the lamplight
gnats dance a double helix;
someone is singing by a forest stream,
young girls are washing
in a forest stream.

Blind Tiger, these traps were not set by us;
we did not give our consent.

ix

Blind Tiger you are a foolish god
but our foolishness is greater.

The noise of helicopters
is shaking the dead in their graves,
and children too young to know,
wake startled
by the sound of something
quite inexplicable.

How can the celandine
justify its existence;
as the season rots,
as spring rots;
we shake our heads
with the making of it?

x

Who carves you in amber
singing to the trees,
singing to the woman
who breaks bark
revealing the heart wood,
the pith which carries
both water and sun?

I watch the flames
through your eyeholes;

watch the flames
through your tear-shaped nostrils.

After love, after beauty,
once the spirit passes,
nothing remains but fire.

Nicola Warwick

They all look like Pegasus

Maybe it's their gleamy flanks
and the way they appear
like spectres from the mist.

Maybe it's the slow turn of the head,
the lift of muzzle from grass
when all you've done is whistle.

Or the way that in every light
they look see-through. The way winter
thickens their coats to plumage.

The way some look as if they're
ready for flight at the sudden
bark of a dog, a gunshot.

Perhaps it's the way a bar of sunlight
blurs their outlines, gives them wings,
feathers their manes.

And they're so calm on the halter
and look at you with a trusting glance
as if saying *You know who I am.*

Jessica Mookherjee

Lascaux Cave

Folding rock becomes
liquid, becomes solid.
It is all the same to her.
She gapes and grins
from every orifice
as they
paint her calluses and
ingrained skin.
Inside her it is hot and dank
and lit
by animal fat that
becomes her tattoos.
The never-maiden holds
her bellicose breath then
whispers to her shaman
in gibberish, the secrets
to keep the horses running.

Paul Connolly

Bede's Bird

Pace good Bede, we did not enter. All thresholds
Are consequential, bind what was before to now.
We arrived here without an advent and may go
Without a terminus. If we could not behold

Our *in* through customary retrospection's door,
What will be our *out* when we might not pass through it?
Bede's bird can only match us, if it comes and quits
The room insensate, hatched out cold upon the floor.

Elizabeth Barton

Feather

I found it in a field –
a kestrel's feather, beaded

with dew and as I picked it up
it stirred a wildness deep within me.

I was struck by its bold design –
cream and chestnut barbs tigered

with brown, the way its shaft traced
the curve of my palm like a life line

and I thought: *what I'd give for a taste
of the kestrel's short, fierce life.*

I looked up and longed
for the sight of a falcon folding

the world in her fiery embrace,
head still, wings flickering,

her fantail tipped with light
and on my way home

the feather sang
like a hollow reed

summoning me
from this shadow life

to open sky,
a pen to write with

Gorse

When Swedish botanist,
Carolus Linnaeus, first came to England
and saw the gorse in bloom
it's said he fell to his knees in wonder –
perhaps it was the scent of coconut, the sight
of prickly spires with gaudy yellow mouths like snagged
sunlight, that made him glad to be alive.

Since then, we've banished it
to the ragged edges of our minds
but the gorse keeps rising, sulphurous spikes
erupting from ditches, breaching
the banks of the motorway, needling us
with memories of a harsher age when the land was wild and open
and gorse crackled in our hearths.

The Hibernating Heart

This house is too cold since you left
I've sealed every vent
curled up in bed
in a nest of feathers and fleece
but the chill won't lift.

I miss your homecoming –
the anticipation I used to feel
as your brake lights pulsed in the dark
and the kitchen blind
burned scarlet

but now I slide the chain across the door
too early; there's a scar
in our bed where you used to sleep.
At night, your absence haunts me –
it growls in my ear, I can feel
its breath on my neck.

Outside, spring bleeds
into existence –
red buds burst from the twigs
of the Japanese quince and the plum tree
but in here it's always winter
as though my heart's locked in a torpid sleep
in a dark chamber, its veins
clotted with ice.

Will Burns

Heavy Weather

The noise that cracked
us was two or three miniature motorcycles,
a noise from out of doors,
like the bees we let die.

There were rubber boats
in the news and no borders to heavy weather
wherever you were.
And those few weeks

after your birthday, the last of summer
was when the bone-cold
came on us.

They said it would come,
a rain like this. We're up late
with one of your coughing fits.

A good job
the morning has nothing
but its stale echo of night.
No work any more, no tasks.

Sarah Parker

Windswept

All I have is
an image of
windswept trees

as I see in flight
to Parma

that the shimmer
of sound we brought
to the air is gone

and far below on the hillside
shape bended and sculpted
a windswept tree

rises to sight you

then landed in Parma

Italian voices drift clamour
and a strange pure peace
seeks to bring me to solace

and so I catch
a flash to flight

where leaves break
the breeze into
arboreal speech

and I see my self
firm to fracture
into uncertain paths

as now I feel the
sound strength of
windswept trees.

Karen Dennison

Waterloo Bridge

Remember the winter of '99,
standing on Waterloo Bridge;
how a windstorm threatened
to juggle us in its shadow-puppet
theatre of air.

In the Little Ice Age, the Thames
would freeze, ice lodged
in its closely-spaced piers. Frost fairs
grew like crystals: skating rinks,
shops, dancing reels, spit-roasted ox.

Now the river's just-ironed denim,
bleach-streaked with the lights
from Westminster Bridge
and the Wheel's a ruby ring,
sprinkling a patch of sequin-pink.

I'd forgotten how London
is part of my skin, an invisible tattoo
of the time we spent,
the vertiginous thrill
of its backbone of bridges.

We clung to each other that day
with a rigor mortis grip, spoke
of the ice floe that broke away,
devouring people and tents;
joked of being swallowed whole,

sinking down to the city's silted bones
– how we'd never let each other go.

Henry St Leger

Muse

Sitting straight up I aimed for the moon
with a hand and asked a question,
saying I hadn't worn my shoes in

and hung so long my wrist committed suicide,
the everywhere ink
drying, like a crime scene.

But my figure must have cut too well,
because my skirts distracted the boys
who ran, stumbling, into their own new shoes,

with feet that could barely kick,
and Leonard Cohen was a
greaser who wanted to fuck me to church music,

until I was perpetually teenage-pregnancied
unsupported on the library desk, gnarling
you could feel the feet kick to China

the heels were so,

and the stillborn was a mess
of indistinct markings and lesions,
the same capital vowel

gashed over and over again, as if
the new girl had let herself loose
on the operating table

looking for gloss
on her undersides
like in the waiting room magazines.

Isabel Galleymore

Like Double

Am I made like double cream?
Do I grow a second storey
as dough that rises in the heat
or do I move more quickly –
chimera'd in this way do I
try out new wings and talons,
or am I like a bee that bears
my own small weight in pollen?
Tonight two people stand
and lean their heads together:
a wishbone's hinge that wonders if
the wish is in their fracture.

Pronghorns

One blade of grass lifts oddly
as an eyebrow in the bush
and the pronghorns are off –
second to leopards in their speed
that's so unnecessary,
sprinting from what once chased them
that was chased out itself –
teeth and claws constructed
from the air we breathe, is it
like what follows me here,
making of my body
clumsier running.

Antony Mair

Some Things Don't Change

They gave me lace-up brogues that shone like conkers –
too big at first, and I slipped on the insole, but
I liked to please, so wore them, and my feet
grew into their form. When I left home, though,

they began to pinch. A blister appeared
on my heel. I bought some tasselled loafers,
in which my foot spread comfortably.

When visiting my parents I polished the brogues
and squeezed my feet into them. My toes
pressed against the end. I was glad to leave.

I never threw the brogues away. Even now,
when you look at me in a certain way, I notice
that even though I know you love me
I've put them on again.

Charlie Baylis

A Park in Barcelona

Federica, I am in Barcelona

Perhaps you have visited? Armed with your mother and stormy weather.

Perhaps you have visited this park? – it is famous. Green and gold dust, blue shrubs and virgin light.

Perhaps you have sat on this very bench – it is not impossible

Perhaps you have sat on this bench, dreamt up my name and smiled, someone you had yet to meet, but part of your future, a small part (it would seem)

Because when I sit here I think of you

Empress of the soft roads, siren, with long brown curls and saucer eyes

Federica, did I ever tell you I met your father? I met him and complained of your conduct: the constant chatter, the irrepressible need for attention, though I was the same, or similar

The azure of the sky paints a swirl in your eye

I've fallen in love with you, a love that is impossible. Your heart is Rossetti's singing bird,
your lips will always flutter, your future mapped out by nightingales and fairytales

Butterfly, fleur de lys, I wonder what you think of me – older, stranger, a poet of sorts, a fool if anything

Federica, it is not fair how you tease me, telling me you love me, sending me kisses, I know you're just being silly

I insist on propriety

You are young and you will marry

Federica, you will not marry me

*

Federica, clasp and lift a cup of velvet sadness. Co-codamol clouds, Capulet in gowns

Dream of gold ripples dancing on an ocean of tears (ballades without sounds)

So many of my poems carry your F, your E, your D...

And all of them strike the same melancholic note – of a wish that can never be

I want you to have every single joy, Federica

I want you to always be in love, a love that is as strong as love's first bite, or stronger, a love that lasts forever – even if it is not with me

And I hope you come to Barcelona

And find my thoughts, here where I leave them, here where I let it all lie

On this bench – in a famous park

Where I write, adrift in a turbulent world, anchored by thoughts of you, Federica.

Black magic

If, tonight, we have the correct moons
we can synchronise the oscillation of the sea
with the step of the elephant, with the step of the bride
holding a melting glass of cyan

if, tonight, the stars are luminous
we will wake to streets of petals, panthers
strolling around our cemetery beds, if we have matches
we will have glitter, for the witches dancing on the fingertips

of fingertips we will burn flowers on the beaches
breathing the blue smoke of sickness
from the bellies of mute matadors, twisting
their necks around the empty taverns, I want to drip

indigo bruises onto your silk eyelashes
and sew your lips shut with a silver thread
in silence, so we can wrap the night around us
savouring the lost magic of its claws

Sasha Dugdale

The Daughter of a Widow

From my birth I had heard those words
As a small child I saw them from her lips

And learnt them myself. 'Killed in the war'
But having known no absence they were shapely

Trailing, veil-thin, through the glass and grit
Which had by then permeated through alveoli

Entered the bloodstream, lodged in the fingertips.
No one may know that which is death,

Before their time, and I saw only that
Which is elderly before its time, disappointment.

She had no more knowledge than I, how he
Was hit, by whom, and was he thinking of her

Like that mortally wounded man who, smiling, asked the nurse
To open her gown and show him her breasts

Because he had not seen his wife for nearly a year.
Unhappy woman, she rushed from his bed as he reached

And only returned when he was dead
She remembers, old now, thinking always of the breach,

How the same smile played around his lips in death.

Stephen Noon

xxii

Writing |
by way of multiplex (the uncut). Because the pain of infinite singing
not slayeth
this time; this time
let us
the fullness of all song. Phoebus of the thick hair, singing
the number of sand.
Pain
endures | endures
jaw: my *tabernaculum* for whorl
of
livid jewel.

Tim Liardet

The Flint-rasp

I am involved in an industry which argues that individuals can be *taught* to write poetry. Many teachers of writing – including myself – are autodidacts. There are autodidacts attempting to do for others what was never done for them: helping others to learn how to shape, extend and complete their poems, how to channel bottomless hunger into a mean mould on the page. In writing departments there are autodidacts attending the assembly line. Anyone with even the remotest taste for ironising irony would like this one. At poetry workshops up and down the country, in a range of highly distinguished university writing departments, poets are being taught how not to be autodidacts. To be taught, the *gestalt* of poetry needs to be broken down into its constituent *grasps*. The danger of this process is incalculable and possibly self-evident. What can survive, if the tutor is not vigilant, the excessive, often consensual pruning of the group? What can grow when the poem has been ruthlessly cut back to facilitate new growth?

There is something Darwinian in this process: the weaker parts must give way to the stronger and, because the poem's destiny is shaped by the same judges who have been taught to speak the same critical language, the eighteen poems written by the eighteen members of the workshop might display an alarming uniformity of tone. Even uniformity of shape. Even uniformity of subject matter. At times, I fear I might be in the business of creating norms. Because so many undergraduate poems suffer from the same ailments, these are the elements that get most rigorously addressed: the imbalance between the provision and withholding of too much information, mystery and disclosure; the assumption on the part of the poet that the reader was present at the birth of his or her last thought; the wayward dowsing for the active verb, without finding it; the absence of any controlling perception at all; the setting up – and subsequent failure to achieve – resolution. All these have to be addressed so carefully that I am concerned at times that all we do is set up a sort of column of tick-boxes for the complete poem, entirely defined by the shortfall of work coursing through the system. This means, perhaps, the needs of individual poems and students are met, but at the expense of what? I do feel a range of newly published collections are the pressed-out product passing through the hands that wear rubber gloves before dropping into the deep baskets, bound for the public spaces.

And who are Creative Writing students? Attempting to teach poetry to the inmates of the second largest Young Offenders' Prison in Europe taught me they weren't behind bars. Often, it seems, teaching the southern bourgeoisie in the sunlit rooms of a southern university (whose every square inch of tended grass and Bath stone is owned by the Duchy) poses problems not dramatically different. Every year a huge bank of youthful bristling energy is fed through the faculty. A small minority of undergraduates who go for the poetry option are already secretly unmoved by it and do not quite feel equal to the task of understanding it, let alone writing it. A similar percentage are also existentially unengaged, perhaps, even when doing something that might otherwise interest them. They might even regard a three hour seminar, in which they are expected to contribute intelligently, with appropriately mastered forms of critical language, as a certain sort of sentence. The poetry modules become a kind of soft option, preferable in many ways to the harsher disciplines, say, of history or politics. Glimpsed at a distance, there'd be no right or wrong answers – the poetry modules might seem to offer infinite scope for abundant subjectivity.

There are of course many serious students. A majority of these are, they argue, far too busy writing their own poems to have time to read the work of professional poets. A percentage of that majority clearly opt for Undergraduate Creative Writing to be 'discovered' – the moment individuals realise this may not necessarily happen quickly tests the mettle of their commitment. If they persevere at this point, promise can be sustained. Having been told of the eerie protocols of the poetry world and not having been deterred, there may be some hope they might be tentatively guided, perhaps, to the fulfilment of their potential. What is striking at this stage is the handing over of trust into the hands of their tutor. In my case, this is the handing over of trust into the hands of the autodidact – trust is given in this way much more readily than it is given to the group as a whole. Many students assume their peers have not matured sufficiently to criticise their work. Conversely, there are those who flagrantly prefer to remain autodidacts – they stay at home, writing poems to themselves and duly hand in their coursework on submission day without once having attended a seminar. The obvious point about such students is that there is often a marked autodidactic element in their work – talent that doesn't want to put itself at risk. The tutors mark it with impartiality, even when he or she has not been regarded as a source of help or inspiration.

What I look for in student work is originality. The flint-rasp of sparks, most likely to have flown in the prison. Tracers in the dark. Vocabulary that fizzes. Vision that is true, and language that can hold it still enough on the page. The critic, Harold Bloom, rejects the view, I recall, of a handing over from precursor to student poet. Trope reverses trope which reverses cause and effect. Originality is the moment of freedom which all would-be-poets must

49

achieve by creating discontinuity and the illusion of origins. 'Weak' poets accept the handing over of tutorial advice and are silenced by it; 'strong' poets react against it, swerve away from the precursor, and rewrite the parent influence in such a way that, far from appearing influenced by the earlier, the later poet now appears to have created the earlier poet's work. The moment all tutors look for in a student is what Bloom calls the moment of self-begetting: some regard this as the achievement of a distinctive voice, perhaps, the breakthrough into mastery of the line: the poet has to 'overhear' and work through the ghostly echoes or allusions which haunt him/her until the point at which quotation/plagiarism becomes self-begetting: the point at which the poet does not steal or synthesize but speaks for her/himself.

Even when teaching at postgraduate level this moment is not as frequent as most might hope. But when it is glimpsed, it is often associated with a newfound begrudging of the tutor's 'wisdom'. The 'parental' aspect of the creative relationship is never very far away. Often, as far as I can work out, something like the moment of begetting comes six months after the end of the course of study, when all new awarenesses of art and self have been thoroughly distilled. Even when actively 'taught', a talented student only learns what he /she finally teaches him/herself. In a typical tutorial, perhaps, all we can hope for is intersubjectivity: the crucible of the student's personal fear, resentment, self-doubt and growing confidence mixed in with the tutor's attempted solicitude and deliberate interrogation; at which stage, perhaps, each person involved is an autodidact.

Carol Rumens

Can you Teach Verse-Writing?

Defining 'verse' in the broad sense, from metrical and syllabic structures to the looser asymmetric patterns favoured by many contemporary poets, the answer is yes, usually. I've taught verse-writing techniques to university students for a number of years, now, and at widely differing institutions. Total lack of verbal ability is rarer than special talent, in fact. Many students can be taught to write a better than adequate sonnet: most can produce a free-verse narrative using lines and stanzas for interesting syntactic and dramatic effects. All can write short, imagistic verse, finding good words and a pleasing order in which to place them.

This is not to claim that anyone has the potential to be an original genius, a new Dickinson or Hopkins or Reznikoff. All we're aiming for is a certain level of competence in versification – which, in essence, is lineation (formal and otherwise), the apt deployment of rhythm, metaphor, imagery and narrative, the ability to hear words and lines melodically. Students may also be shown how to use visual, spatial effects on the page. This is attainable by anyone with normal cognitive function, language fluency and willingness to work.

Most first-year English students arrive poorly prepared to study literature or literary writing: they have read little, their sentence-construction is shaky, their vocabulary limited. But their work will be close-read and they will be expected to revise it. They'll read as many fine poems as time allows in the two-semester, one-hour-per-week seminar. They'll begin by thinking birthday-card jingles and rock lyrics are poetry, or that the essence of poetry is 'self-expression.' By the end of the course, they'll have a sense of the importance of language itself. All will write more vividly, interestingly, logically, originally than at the beginning. A good proportion will pass the assessment with a mark in the fairly good (C) to very good (B+) range.

If this account sounds worthy or lacklustre, the experience is not. Almost every poetry-course yields real poems, pieces which are somehow alive beyond their technical competence, or alive despite its lack. A lot depends on the student's willingness to be weaned off the cliché, including the clichéd rhyme. Most are willing and even enjoy fine-tuning their cliché-sensors. To know and scorn the sleep-inducing catch-phrase, to value clarity and favour particularity, is to attain acts of thought as well as poetry. Outside the predictive text-box of the literature essay the student takes full responsibility for his or her words. In any future job, this should still be an advantage.

To versify and thereby intensify language is not a radically different matter from learning to speak it. But poets know that words can be too solid and convincing; we need to love them and distrust them. We have to recognise our own susceptibility to them as well as noting their betrayal by politicians – something the young may readily do. There's a complex morality in poetry, an art which, although very clearly more than mere self-expression, is directly rooted in the bodily self. 'Tell the truth, but tell it slant.' Tell a lie, but tell it true. And make sure it's *your* lie, not someone else's.

The worst offence of state education is the under-exploitation of children's natural facility for language. I'm not referring to the failure to teach other languages effectively, although that is thoroughly regrettable, but the failure to teach children their own. Creative Writing, at its most basic, is an extension of literacy-learning, and includes the self-respect, the liberation, of knowing oneself fully literate.

Indulge me in a trip to the Classroom of Memory. At my primary school, we suffered regular spelling-tests and English dictations. We wrote a 'composition' every week – sometimes an essay in the genre now called Creative Non-Fiction ('My Summer Holiday') but mostly an exercise in something now called Creative Writing ('A Day in the Life of a Penny'). We learnt poems by heart and recited them dolorously. We copied texts which the teacher had chalked, squeaking and crumbling, onto the blackboard (I recall a laborious session with Blake's 'Little Lamb, who made thee?' and my total confusion about the word 'dust' when spelt with an 'o'). About once a year we got to write a poem of our own.

At the age of 11, I was given a copy of Palgrave's *Golden Treasury*. I read it over and back and in and out: I bought a notebook and imitated some of the more emotive styles. Sunsets, Cupid and the River Derwent featured with lamentable frequency in my inventively titled Golden Book of Poetry. My favourite poet was Milton. I loved the sound and colour of his Latinate diction; not understanding what the hell he meant didn't bother me in the least. I was a dreamy pre-teen lifted on the rolling waves of verbal passion (a dangerous, but probably inevitable, condition). So I began my Creative Writing course – which I have not so far completed.

People sometimes have a romantic notion of the untutored, ready-born poetic genius, but the facts are otherwise: every poet whose work is remembered today took lessons. He might have translated Homer from the Greek, at Eton or Winchester, or he might have left school early but lucked out with a schoolmaster-friend who recognised his half-educated talent and read him Chapman's Homer. He might have stuck poems on whin bushes, like Patrick Kavanagh, so he could glance at them as he trudged about the fields of his impoverished small farm: he might have idled away a Tudor courtier's leisure-time by organising sonnet-contests. That is, he did an apprenticeship.

Creative Writing has always been taught, and theorised about. The discourse begins, as far as we know, with Aristotle's *Poetics*. It took the forms of Rhetoric, Classical Prosody and Translation for poets of the schools and universities of the Renaissance. Importantly, it has always flowed over the pedagogic borders, to include informal personal reading, the exchange of work with friends, the rivalry of peers and the wisdom of mentors. This Higher Education in Creative Writing education, unlike today's £9,000 per annum package, was free of charge, at least at point of purchase.

Such luxury was not available to everyone. You were well advised to be born an upper-class male. You attended public school (Greek and Latin de rigueur), and thence to Oxford or Cambridge for the Trivium. To be the daughter of a successful man with a rather fine library was the next best thing – but, alas, poor blue-stocking, you would have the texts without the travel, the trouble, the sex, drugs and rock 'n roll to fire your learning and allow you to make brilliant books of your own. (There were happy exceptions, of course: Elizabeth Barrett Browning was one of the happiest).

There's no reason why an academic Creative Writing course should exclude the valuable informal elements of the posh boys' poetry-club. I encourage students to have a writing life beyond the timetable. Many of them need little encouragement, since the informal collaborative exercises, like the Tan-Renga, usually spark the shy into further connection. There are poets' visits and public readings. And, of course, the mixed blessing of the Internet.

The really interesting question may not be *can* verse-writing be taught? but *how* should it be taught? Can it be fitted into the formal educational structure without distortion?

I firmly support the modular system for English undergraduates. And I believe the two Creative Writing modules (prose and poetry) should be part of the non-elective core. Students, in any event, have to be writers: let them practise writing, then, and explore the variety of possible genres and styles. (It will improve their essays!) Conversely, I would prohibit degree-courses which consisted purely of Creative Writing, with no study of historical texts. In an ideal literature course, there would be modules in modern poetry and fiction to complement the creative modules, and tutors would co-operate on an integrated reading and writing plan. Reading has by far the most crucial role in anyone's learning to write.

Creative Writing does not fit comfortably into the curriculum. Treated like any knowledge-centred subject, with gradated blocks of information to absorb and be tested on, it's beset with targets and rubrics. 'By the end of the semester the student will be able to...' – well, what? I always feel like quoting Peter Levi's wonderful book, *The Noise Made by Poems*: the student will be able 'to hear words as an 18th century sailor heard every creak and groan of his ship'... (apologies for the paraphrase).

Then there's the dreaded assessment, the assessment-sheet and the assessment grid, and the little box for the approving words and the little box for the could-do-better bullet points. I hate bullet points. In fact I hate a lot about marking. I hate the categorical method because the distinctions are crude: numerical marking at least allows you to distinguish a 52% from a 53. I hate having to mark online: my sensitivity to words seems entwined with my eye-hand coordination, and my thoughts about poetry curl naturally into cursive. I hate the charade of anonymity: I know my students' work pretty thoroughly by the time they get to hand it in. I hate the fact that they are obliged to write a 'self-reflective commentary'. Although I do want them to be self-reflective, I'd rather not be told about it, especially when it's a matter of puffery or overdone apology. Creative Writing needs to be assessed, of course, but that process should be continuous and include an evaluation of development. There may have to be the simple, credit-earning categorisations of Pass and Pass with Merit – but, in the meantime, the tutor will have commented productively on everything the student has written, and the poems will have been revised. The academy needs to understand that taste is a serious factor in the aesthetic judgement which CW assessment fundamentally is. They should not disdain taste.

It's unfortunate that the universities brought in so many writers when CW was laying the golden recruitment egg, and then screwed up the kinds of teaching we had to offer. They wanted more lesson-plans and less staring into imaginative space. Some wanted to dictate the lesson-plan. Universities know little about contemporary poetry, but they know they favour the avant garde (it's food for research), and fail to see the folly of teaching students to smash the icon before they know what an icon is.

Finally, there's the question of what should be taught. Students writing poetry need to read the 20th century 'classics'– Yeats, Auden, Stevens, Larkin, Bishop. We should include newly published contemporary poets, too. The quality is bound to be variable, but this doesn't matter: it's useful for students to investigate what's being written now, and to do so with critical alertness. Other important elements of the course are exercises, sometimes playful and improvised, reading aloud and, of course, discussion. The ideal is a delicate balancing between close-reading an exemplary text and close-reading the student's own piece of writing.

The question of the poet or novelist in the university is bound up with the question of non-specialist teaching. Its opponents should not assume that there is less rigour than in the historical modules. We even bother to correct the grammar! But, more significantly, we engage with our students as whole people, valuing the memories, voices, idiolects they bring to their poems. It's easy to patronise students, but poetry insists we meet them as human equals. They teach us as much as we teach them. They remind us that the last word is never said, the trick never explained. Beginning a new poem, every writing-professor becomes a fresher.

John F Deane

Workshops

Over eight or nine successive summers, I directed a poetry workshop in The Joiner Centre of the University of Massachusetts in Boston. The Centre was founded as a focal point for the study of war and its social consequences, basically by veterans of the Vietnam War. Each year there was an exchange between Boston and Hanoi, between veterans of that war from either side. The poetry workshop was aimed at veterans but open to adults who were interested in writing poetry. I took my 'teaching' very seriously, and so did the participants. I promised each participant that he or she would have a new, publishable poem by the end of the two weeks. And it worked. I developed a technique for producing a poem out of the individual tasks I set at each session, building from a simple base (differing with each person as I insisted on exact physical description of a person's chosen locale) through several clearly-defined steps. They thought I was great! But I soon came to know that the technique offered, while I was able to draw out the 'poem' by close attention to each individual's efforts, most of the writers were unable to write further work, even using the actual learned technique, without my presence. So each year I had to start anew, though the same individuals frequently reappeared. It is easy, I have learned, to teach technical things; it is impossible to teach inspiration, deep response to the music of language, the relevance to an individual of the depth of his or her world-view (*Weltanschauung*) and how to probe its actuality and its mystery, and then how to see the world through metaphor and image.

In a poem by Lao Tzu, written many centuries ago, are the words: 'instrument and voice achieve one harmony'. A further phrase of Lao Tzu reads: 'listening and not hearing it, I will call it inaudible'. And this I interpret as a failure to be present to our living, a failure of awareness of what the world presents in our lives and thoughts, and if I fail such presence, I seek excuses for my failure. The words I constantly keep before my mind are 'permeable' and 'impermeable'. My greatest fear in living and in working towards poetry, is that I impose my will and thoughts on the world around me, rather than allowing the reality and the mystery of the world come through to me. You cannot teach, in a workshop, how to become 'permeable'.

Too often, after voluminous notes, the gathering of words, phrases, images, the fire of inspiration does not catch. It is then that I fear that I am trying to net the mysteries, and the mysteries will not be netted; I am trying to name the name that bears no name. I am imposing; I am not listening. It is like in prayer: the tendency for a believer to chatter away to God, pleading, begging, praising... and rarely listening. It is in the emptying of self that the mysteries will approach and in this way I see the good poet as a kind of mystic, even a prophet. You cannot teach, in a workshop, how to pray, how to 'listen'. It is the high esteem in which I hold poetry that continues to astonish me, and to frustrate me; and it is even more frustrating to hope, and to try, to get this across to others as too often I find myself a failure in the work.

The one thing that is certain, and that is most difficult, is that a poem will not be forced into existence. So, after much labour, after several re-visionings of the work, the experience, the thought, the language, after much re-drafting, it is painful yet honest to dump the thing, if it does not cohere. A poem catches fire by a deserved, a worked-for moment of intuition, when that moment comes with the words that earth the insight. That miracle. You cannot teach, in workshops, how to perform the miracle.

The outcome of every effort at a poem is, therefore, still doubtful. The work for me always takes root in one of two things: either a small (sometimes great) excitement over the encounter with a moving or beautiful part of the earth about me, or an insight – garnered from reading or simply listening to my own thinking – into what I am searching for, the meaning of our living. It will take not an *either/or* to make a poem, it will take a *both/and*, at least two shoots to develop, and a greater poem if there are more than that, more branches and leaves that make the one eucalyptus tree. It is not that the physical world about us is merely described, though this I do constantly, trying to figure why an event or a thing seen will excite, and this I try to catch always through the surging of the language that might echo the original emotion. Nor is it that I will add a seam of thinking to that physical image. The process is a complex one and will develop, or not, over a period of days, or weeks, or longer. The fear is that the unitive in-breathing inspiration will not occur, that a mere single flame will fizzle up and out, without the conflagration of a good poem. You cannot stay with, and help develop, another writer over a long enough period of time, while understanding and encouraging their deepest being.

I know that, even if I have succeeded in writing a handful of pieces that I would fairly confidently call 'poems', I still have not come near to writing the poem that I believe is really in there somewhere, the poem that says it all, that sings it all, that clarifies and deepens all to its full reason and its complete being. And I know, too, such success cannot be taught in workshops.

Gill McEvoy

Creative Writing?

Do you really need a BA or an MA in Creative Writing to be a writer or poet? Paper and pen is surely good enough – or a laptop if you prefer it. It is true that you might find a mentor kind enough to promote you and your work into the limelight on such a course but only if you yourself show a talent that is outstanding. Meanwhile the real writer is at home, head down, writing.

You can no more teach someone to be a writer than you can teach someone to be a brilliant cook. You can show them the forms, the examples of style, plot and genre, but, unless that spark and drive is already there, little will happen.

What you can do, however, is open up a new world to students, helping them to see the world another way, to discard conversational clichés and find new ways of speaking, help them to look at an object and see not merely a pebble but a whole geological history or a vast range of extraordinary patterns. Which is marvellous for all concerned – and very hard work for you.

It's certainly a useful way for poets/other writers to earn some real money, and a useful source of income for universities, some of whom no doubt do see the remarkable emerge from their tutoring. But for those writers who undertake to do this sort of teaching it means a great deal of output and not much input. The danger is that this might interfere with your own creative process.

I have 'taught' Creative Writing at further education level; I loved it, and the students loved it, but I was always aware that I wasn't going to turn out class after class of amazing writers. If that were to have happened I would have been so delighted I'd have danced down the street. It never did but I had the satisfaction of students saying how much they loved my class. Fine, fine. But I'd much rather be at home, head down, writing.

D. V. Cooke

On the Epigoni

For poetry ours is a mediocre age. Never has so much been published under the name of poetry yet nothing stands out against the age. Never have so many prizes been proffered for poetry – awarded as if for and by and to a lesser generation – to the *epigoni* where intellect, vision and sensibility and that natural inborn ability of the English and the English language and what the language itself is capable of has somehow been eliminated or has mysteriously gone missing. Never before has there been so much talk in writing schools and uncreative writing courses regarding poetry – places where poetry itself would never want to stay or linger and where, in general, poetry is talked out of its right and proper existence.

What is needed so that poetry can move forward from the morass into which it has fallen over the past thirty or so years is publishers and editors of intellect, vision and sensibility – each part balanced and mixed to the correct measure, who have more than, as at present, a passing interest in language. These qualities have of late been in rare supply as to become non-existent or an endangered species. A situation which has led to there being much – too much poetry in the lower to middle range but hardly any poetry being written from the middle to higher levels. There is virtually nothing of what Matthew Arnold called *the grand style* being written or published. What is being written, taught and published is of the low style. There is also very little quality poetry published now from any publisher for thinking people or for people who are conscious and aware of that which the English language is capable of. If you are looking for that much talked about thing – a gap in the market (rather a gaping hole these days), then there does exist such a rare commodity. It is for quality poetry for educated readers. What *is* being published by our large and not so large poetry publishing companies for the most is mainly a triumph of marketing over poetry – a kind of faux poetry that panders to and services the overspill from Creative Writing courses whose motto might be: poetry minus the imagination, or – poetry you don't have to think too much about. After all, Shakespeare did not need to aspire to the heights of a Creative Writing course to be able to write, but merely attained a good Grammar School education which seemed ample and more than sufficient to his needs. John Milton also seemed amply content with his own self-enforced and self-administered reading of the classics. So much so that in his tract *Of Education* he recommends rather than, forcing the empty wits of children to compose theme, verses, and orations, they might acquire the life of virtue by much reading of the classics. However, I expect as things are – perhaps we shall shortly be able to begin to think about what heights and expression of language both Shakespeare and Milton might have achieved if they had only attained a place on a Creative Writing course.

Who then is there to be admired? Who should the aspirant read? Well of course they must read *Agenda*. Yet to go forward we must clear the mind and go back to begin at a beginning. There we might find Donne, Marvell and Herbert who put some thought and figure into poetry. Empson – poet and critic, who showed how poetry and language worked. Eliot (T.S.) for his formal intellect and critical and moral intelligence allied to an outstanding ear for rhythms inherent in the language as she is yet spoken. Hopkins for his listening to and dedication to the poetic pulse (who lost faith in Tennyson and came in time to outdistance Tennyson), who, though unknown in the age he lived through, did not unduly overcare if his poems were read but by a few – only that they were written for the grandeur and glory of God. And above all Shakespeare for his inborn facility with language where one image proceeds out of another and character arises from character – for his dramatic invention and for his natural innate ability which contained and far outdistanced all others. Milton for his grandeur and design – his architectonics and ability to interweave Greek and Latin classics into English poetry. Pope for his wit and sudden turn and reversals of phrase. And numerous others who move the language about a bit; who imbue poetry with rhythm and meaning; who take joy in working in and with the English language; who sometimes find it necessary to dislocate its syntax to make its meaning clear – who through the ages have crafted and constructed the English poetic canon.

As opposed to the creation of this central English canonical tradition, the rise of Creative Writing courses is more to do with the decline and failure of English Education to teach pupils to write or express themselves succinctly or correctly rather than any desire to produce great literature. I've never seen a poem come out of Creative Writing schools that is worthy of the English language – each takes more from the language than it gives. A kind of one-legged poetry that has to be propped up by prizes – that adds little if anything to the sum of human knowledge or to the greater glory of the language. Each book allocated and given a prize; nobody must fail; each book published to service the vanity of the market. The Forward Prize, the T. S. Eliot Prize, et al. (Would T.S. Eliot have won the T.S. Eliot prize?) Are the recipients of these and others the best that mankind has to offer? Isn't even the thought of poetry written for prizes to misunderstand the nature of poetry? Prizes are mostly to do with who's in and who's out, and are no indication of *quality* or the outcome of a critical mind but are to do with power groupings within the so-called poetry world; they almost always go to the wrong person or wrong book and are more an indication of the clique who, at any one time, by whatever means, have gained power and control of the market. Yet the list of poetry books and pamphlets published each year grows and groans in dullness. Over two thousand a year now in this country alone, each containing poetry which for the most falls dead from the pen or printer – that has no life-giving energy or canonical thought but lives in the darkness of illusion. The manufactured and bubble reputations which are there to serve the merely contemporary; which neither inform nor instruct nor give pleasure – intellectual or sensory; which will not be read in another ten years or fifty years or a hundred years; which are there to satisfy the vanity of the writer and the Creative Writing industry that they have done something worthwhile in that forever lost and yet undiscovered country of poetry. If, one by one, these courses could be closed down and the energy expended therein sent to more deserving places, then English poetry would be much the richer both in thought, imagination and language.

However, the aspirant should not yet give up hope. Occasionally one may find – as if by accident – a poem that will remind him or her of the magnificence that the language of English Poetry once contained; but these things are generally not encouraged by poetry publishers and have never yet been found in the unrich annals of (un)Creative Writing courses and, if one were to be found, would be frowned on and then politely put down as being elitist and therefore unnecessary to the forward march of mankind. The poetry that has mattered and will matter – to the past, present and future – doesn't need Creative Writing courses and prizes and awards but is self-evident what it is and always has been: its own self perfectly alive within its own life that goes on indeterminate – seeping into the consciousness of the race and nation, sometimes making itself known to the conscious mind, other times working quietly away in the unconscious regions. That is the poetry English publishers should be publishing and which (un)Creative Writing courses will never teach.

Tony Curtis

Poets Teaching Poetry

The sharing of creative processes and the teaching, formal and informal, of the creative arts is central to our civilization. From Socrates and Plato, through Wordsworth and Coleridge, Owen and Sassoon, Pound and Eliot to Lowell and Plath, in prose and poetry the sharing of ideas and words, even the incorporation of another writer's ideas and strategies, has been crucial to the establishment and development of many of our most significant writers. Writing is of necessity an essentially solitary practice, but which of us has not wished for an intimate early reader or mentor at times?

I went to Swansea University in the autumn of 1965 and began to write poetry and take that activity more seriously, more centrally, over the next three years. You would imagine that the role and example of Swansea's greatest poet, the country's greatest poet would have been an early influence, but that was far from the case. Dylan Thomas was not mentioned by our lecturers, even on the Modern British and American course for which I'd opted. He'd died thirteen years before, so perhaps it was all a bit raw; Kingsley Amis had just left the staff and, no doubt, they'd had too much of larger-than-life writers. Though the English Society did have a steady trickle of fascinating guests – the Irish poet W.R. Rogers, the suave and seductive Dannie Abse, that breaker of fiction boundaries B.S. Johnson (I still have his unbound and meant-to-be-shuffled novel-in-a-box, *The Unfortunates*, in my glass bookcase). There was also a reading by Kathleen Raine, another poet invited to do a reading tour of America by John Malcolm Brinnin, though hardly in the staggering steps of Dylan. She was impressively mystifying and spoke of only recognising 'true poets' such as Vernon. She was the guest of Vernon Watkins who, in the academic year 1966/67 had been invited to the university as Gulbenkian Fellow. Recently retired as 'the oldest bank clerk in Wales; my father was the youngest bank manager' he was assigned to our 'Modern British and American Literature' course. The trouble was that Vernon, while obviously not American, by birth or inclination, was also problematically British and certainly not Modern. He declared that he could never write a poem that was 'dominated by time'; in his poetry world there could be nothing modern, only ancient truths. Kathleen Raine said that, 'with certainty, he walked on holy ground.'

Vernon Watkins was not a natural teacher of groups so the group shrank: some weeks it was a girl and me, and some weeks just me. The small poet-buds were in me, though I dared not give any indication of this to the

Gulbenkian Fellow and felt honoured to sit at his feet, or on the same bench on campus or in Singleton Park.

This was so long ago and I remember little of what was said, except that here was a Faber poet, someone who had signed the petition with T.S. Eliot to plead for the traitorous Ezra Pound's life to be spared; the close friend of Dylan Thomas – they had shared drafts of poems with each other, made suggestions and corrections to each other's work, and for whose wedding in 1944 Dylan had not showed up, even though he was supposed to be the best man.

I certainly had no confidence to show Vernon Watkins my poems. Years later I learned that John Ormond had done this when he was an undergraduate at Swansea: the strictures and precise critiquing of his work were so severe that John was shaken from his course as a poet for some years: 'Don't publish anything until you are thirty,' Vernon said. What would Vernon Watkins have made of my student scribblings? I'd had a narrow escape; teaching poets can be dangerous, for both parties.[1]

In Tobias Woolf's novel, *Old School* [2] the narrator explains that his private boys school held literature to be as central as the conventional American goal of team sports. Famous writers were guests of the school and for each visit a competition was held: the best piece of student writing won for that person a personal meeting, a tutorial with Robert Frost or Ernest Hemingway.

> My aspirations were mystical. I wanted the laying on of hands that had written living stories and poems, hands that had touched the hands of other writers. I wanted to be anointed.

The American model is still that: one works to gain a place at an institution which holds a reputation through its faculty. They must be published writers with as many prizes and awards as possible. When you have completed your Masters, you carry their names and that association into your own career. When in 1979 I did the two-year MFA at Goddard College in Vermont working with Stephen Dobyns, Jane Shore and Thomas Lux, I was the only British writer and it took me a couple of residencies to grasp that the first few days of the week-long stay at that wooded campus close to Plainfield, Vermont had better include schmoosing the tutor you'd most like to work with over the following semester. Goddard was a star-studded academy and had particular strengths in drama, a department in which David Mamet had both studied and taught, and photography, as well as in writing. On the

---

[1] See my Mulfran Press book *My Life with Dylan Thomas*, 2014.

[2] Tobias Woolf, *Old School* (London: Bloomsbury, 2004 p.7)

faculty were Louise Glück, Ellen Bryant Voigt, Robert Hass, Michael Ryan, Thomas Lux, Geoffrey Woolf (brother of Tobias) and Donald Hall. Guests in my time included Raymond Carver, Richard Ford and Galway Kinnell. My cohort of students included Mark Doty and his wife who published jointly under the name 'M.R. Doty'. I never did find out whether they graduated with one degree or two.

I returned to Wales and worked to introduce undergraduate writing options on our degree at the Polytechnic of Wales. After ten years these were very well established as free-standing modules and double modules in a diet of English offerings and the MA in Writing was offered in 1993, in what had become the University of Glamorgan. Some five years later this became the M.Phil. in Writing, a more prestigious research degree. Both degrees were predicated on my Goddard experience: two years distance-learning. Candidates had four weekend residencies in each academic year on campus, with a week-long stay in the first summer at the Ty Newydd centre in north Wales. There were eight writers in each cohort and eight tutors. From the beginning, I was keen to involve tutors, both part-time and full-time, who were accomplished writers; these have included Helen Dunmore, Sian James, Gillian Clarke, Philip Gross, Catherine Merriman, Sheenagh Pugh, Chris Meredith, Matthew Francis and Stephen Knight.

The principle of distance-learning was crucial to our postgraduate development: I argued, and still would argue, that a weekly workshop based course anywhere outside a major city can exhaust too quickly the stream of good quality candidates. It is also my view that such courses and workshops are far more suited to poets than fiction writers, though at Glamorgan/South Wales we have had many published and prize-winning writers in both genres.

Of course, the expansion of Creative Writing at UK universities has meant that many writers of real achievement have been able to supplement their very meagre earnings as poets or literary fiction writers with a .5 or .3 post in a local university. This has been of considerable mutual benefit. The students work with a 'real writer', the university secures a proportion of that writer's published work for their REF submission, and the writer keeps free paper in his or her printer and the wolf from the door.

Writing in a 1952 radio broadcast on Edgar Lee Masters, Dylan Thomas reflected on his American campus experiences:

> In poetry workshops, by the way, would-be poets are supposed to study the craft under some distinguished practitioner. Perhaps the original idea was to provide for apprentice poets what a master's studio once did for apprentice painters. But the master painter used to paint all the time, and his apprentices assisted him and were

busy under his direction. A master-poet, if he exists, is supposed, in these literary warrens, to spend nearly all his time dealing with, and encouraging, the imitations, safe experiments, doodlings and batchings of his students, and to do his own stuff on the side. What a pity he does not have the apprentice poets to help him with the duller bits of his own work. There is a future in this, however ghastly.[3]

In this Dylan was as witty as one would expect and more prescient than one might expect. Whilst the model of the painter and his studio may be used to justify the longer tradition of the creative studio or workshop, the principle of subservient collaborative work on a masterpiece will not inform the work of the novelist or poet, I think.

When I stayed on at Swansea to compete my PGCE teaching year, one of our lecturers recommended *English Through Poetry Writing* by Brian Powell (Heinemann 1968), a book aimed at school teachers, the only teachers of writing in those days. The no-nonsense approach of setting students definable tasks after a variety of stimulations proved a successful approach on our teaching practices and, remarkably, for the next forty years. His Introductory Form Stages – Dylan Thomas Portraits, Ezra Pound Couplets, Syllable Poems and Haiku pointing to a composite sequence of all those forms is a sufficient challenge and guide for a wide range of ages and abilities. I have always believed that poetry is writing written in lines; and that is all that distinguishes it from all other forms of writing. Usually the left hand justification is set, and the right hand justification is a mystery known only unto the gods of poetry and the real poet. All the other rhetorical and lyrical strengths of the poet may also be shared by fiction writers, dramatists, preachers and politicians. Asking students to follow the form of, say, the Dylan Thomas Couplet:

Did you ever see an otter?
Sleek-skinned, smooth-sided, fierce-fanged, killer

is asking them to follow the simplest form of two lines (can a one-line poem be a poem? Surely not) and they are being asked to write only one line of their own – a second, completing, answering line and to follow the three double-barrel words and the single word of the completion.

Did you ever see a.......?
---/---,---/----,---/---,---.

---

[3] *Dylan Thomas, Dylan Thomas, The Broadcasts* ed. Ralph Maud (London: Dent & Sons, 1991 p.255)

This sort of game-playing exercise is, of course, limited, but that's the point. As a beginning, a tooling-up of the wanna-be poet or as a limbering-up exercise for the progressing poet, such tricks can be very useful. This may take one into interesting areas from the Junior School up to Starting Poetry One undergraduates. The workshop, small groups of poets with one or more mentoring, is the goal; poems initiated by the students themselves and being sympathetically critiqued by the group with the experienced, published poet at the helm. This is the pinnacle of poetry teaching. At Goddard one had Donald Hall and Louise Glück and their colleagues: that was a challenge and a privilege. That standard of excellence was what I aimed for at Glamorgan. The poem brought to the workshop was respected for its author's intentions and aesthetic, but those could be honestly tried and tested. Let someone else read the poem aloud; how does it sound by a reader other than the poet? What does that reveal about the magic, song, clarity and intrigue of the poem? To the workshop members and to the poet themselves?

At school and undergraduate level, then, I believe there is a place for cold-start stimulation and poem-as-form tasks. I know that my former colleague and Wales National Poet, Gillian Clarke, has used a metaphor game with great effect for many years. Colleagues have employed music, while I have often favoured photographs, a source of my own poems since I began. And also a game of my own which I call 'The Surreal Scissors' which uses a group's random offering of sentence structures – definite article, noun, verb, adverb, preposition, article, noun and then proceeds to move those elements around like a rubric cube until something strange and original is produced. This exercise shakes up presuppositions about imagery, clichés and the conventional narrative. No one poet has ownership of the poem here.

> Slowly the anarchist sleeps under the bell
> Sorrowfully the squirrel sang of the grape
> Blissfully that nun comes by the moorland
> Inevitably the train brings those shells

Well, you get the point, though some students need to be convinced of the muse which chance has introduced them to in such a group.

For over a quarter of a century Dannie Abse (1923-2014) was my friend and poetry mentor, the first reader of my poems (apart from my wife). That is a great privilege, a personal relationship which the best Masters courses and arts councils' mentoring schemes may also lead to and at least in some way seek to emulate. Teaching poetry, teaching the love of poetry is one of the most important things we can do, if we are able. Not all poets want to do that, nor should they feel that reluctance to be a problem. You have to believe in the relationship and the processes of poetry learning; otherwise you'll be unhappy and the student unconvinced.

Though a necessarily small percentage of graduates will publish and become established poets, many others will go on to work in the creative arts in the wider community; and all Creative Writing students of poetry and fiction or drama should become stronger, more committed readers. Perhaps those of us taught by those who were taught by Leavis may still want to believe that they will become better people too.

Mark Wormald

Can you teach Creative Writing? A view from Cambridge

In July 1979, Ted Hughes wrote to the critic Keith Sagar with an account, intended to sound definitive, of a dream that had already acquired the status of a myth. He had long been sharing it, in various forms, with audiences at readings of his work as an introduction to one of the best known of all his poems, 'The Thought-Fox', and over the years some of his friends from Cambridge days had been spreading rumours too, which might have been in danger of developing a life of their own.

In due course he'd go on to describe this dream in a television interview first broadcast in 1988, and featured in 'Stronger than Death', the BBC documentary about Hughes's life and work broadcast in October 2015. He wrote another version of the story for William Scammell's edition of Hughes's 'occasional prose', *Winter Pollen*, in 1994, where it appears to stand guard over, and seems positioned indeed to shadow, the very different story of the poem's genesis that had held generations of school children and their teachers rapt in 'Capturing Animals'. In that wonderful opening talk from 1962, in the series 'Listening and Writing', Hughes had recalled his years of being his elder brother's retriever on hunting expeditions in the valley and moors of his early childhood. Retrievers tend to carry back carcases, and it was Hughes' confession that 'An animal I never succeeded in capturing alive is the fox' that led him swiftly on to the moment when he at last put things to rights: the snowy night in London of the poem's swift and sudden composition, the poem itself – first heard, then, in *Poetry in the Making*, read – and the final crowning claim, not just for that poem itself but for the transcendence of poetry, as a way of happening, capturing, being, over any other form of it, approach to it, way of thinking of it: 'in some ways my fox is better than an ordinary fox. It will live for ever, it will never suffer from hunger or hounds. I have it with me wherever I go. And I made it. And all through imagining it clearly enough and finding the living words' . Hughes has taken possession, not just of the animal, but the words in which it lives and goes on living.

'The fox-dream story really goes as follows,' Hughes told Sagar. And it is much less triumphalist, much more darkly loaded. It relates to a spring night of no snow a little under two years before the night he made famous in *Poetry in the Making*, and I have my own very local and personal reasons for flinching in a curiously conflicted ambivalence whenever I read it. For it couldn't speak more directly to my experience. As Fellow and Director of Studies in English and Senior Tutor at Hughes's Cambridge college, it's hard not to take personally his account of the '*crise*' that beset him during his second year of undergraduate studies in English Literature, and deepened in the midst of a late night essay crisis, his essay on Samuel Johnson with the visitation of a burned fox who places a bleeding paw print on the unwritten page of an essay on Samuel Johnson and urges him to 'Stop this: you are destroying us'. Hughes explains to Sagar, a fellow Cambridge graduate, though of King's not Pembroke College, that he 'connected the fox's demand to my own ideas about Eng. Lit., & the effect of the Cambridge blend of pseudo-critical terminology & social rancour on creative spirit', as expressed through the 'Leavis-style dismantling of texts' – analysis, dismemberment – that seemed to him 'not only a foolish game, but deeply destructive of myself', however talented he knew he was at it. And though there was 'something peculiar to Cambridge at that time that nurtured it, & in particular separated the spirit of surgery & objective analysis from the spirit of husbandry & sympathetic coaching. I don't think it happened at Oxford, for instance.' He took it seriously: took the fox at his word; and 'from that moment abandoned my efforts to adapt myself' to a variety of study and teaching he continued to regard as hostile to the practice of Creative Writing, almost by definition.

Two years afterwards, the foreword to John Fairfax and John Moat's *The Way to Write: a complete guide to the basic skills of good writing* by the co-founders of the Arvon Foundation, whose inaugural national poetry competition he had recently suggested as a means of raising badly needed funds and devoted six months to judging, gave Hughes the chance not just to celebrate the extraordinarily intense psychological transformation that the Arvon course's unique five day immersion in writing alongside a practising poet or writer palpably wrought on its students. It's fascinating to see in this brilliant account of a creative writing's re-engagement with 'the real life of language' and literature the sustained contrast it points up with the resources and effects of 'conventional education'.

> The student is awakened to the real life of language, with all that implies if the physiology of words, their ancestry and history and dynamic behaviour in varying circumstances (of all abbreviated, in conventional teaching, under the heading: grammar). At the same time he is introduced to literature as a living organism, part of the human organism, something which embodies the psychological record of this drama of being alive, something which articulates and illuminates the depth and range and subtlety of being human. Literature becomes as personal to him as his own struggling abilities – no longer, as conventional teaching presents it (and can only present it), a museum of obsolete manners and dead artefacts, without any relevance to 'now and the future'.

And in April 1992, a particularly savage review of his *Shakespeare and the Goddess of Complete Being* in *The Times* by the Cambridge lecturer (and, like Hughes, a graduate of Pembroke) Eric Griffiths led Hughes to return to his theme in an angry letter to the paper's literary editor, and to place the blame at Cambridge's door for a phenomenon he'd first noted with regret 21 years earlier, in that foreword: the disappearance, now treated as the slaughter, of all the creative writing talents Hughes had been spotting amongst the entries he read each summer for the Daily Mirror/W.H.Smith Children's Writing competition. Cambridge English stood squarely in the dock.

I took up my post at Pembroke in October 1992, having just spent seven happy years at Oxford. There I had been a student at Magdalen College, and one of the happiest features of my time there had been exactly that spirit of sympathetic husbandry that two of the College's English Tutors, John Fuller and Bernard O'Donoghue, had brought not just to the study of literature they loved, but also to their own, and to their students' writing. The Florio Society met several times each term in John's room. To attend, you needed to write a poem, always in response to a set theme or form.

For that purpose, extraordinary nerve was required, as an undergraduate, to submit a poem, nearly always in response to a theme, that would need to survive the photocopying and convenor's first reading before the meeting, and then the company of a number of students who were already real poets and have gone on to publish collections: all of them kind but also resolutely honest. Anonymity was a prized principle, and a necessary one, as fundamental to the requirement that only those who had submitted a poem could attend; but submitting did also mean that one's poem had to take its chance of being read too late in a liberally oiled evening to get a reading as sober as one always hoped.

There were, of course, compensations, and not just the poems we got to know and test so well, the vivid sense I have carried with me ever since that poets could and should be critics, that critics should if at all possible be poets, and encourage their students to write.

On my arrival, in Cambridge, I asked whether Pembroke had its own Florio Society. When I heard it didn't, it didn't take me long to decide that it should. I soon decided that the study I'd been allocated, a rather dark but cavernous room above the bar and overlooking the Fellows' carpark, should be its meeting place.

By the time I learned, three years ago, that that first study of mine had, forty years before, been the student bedsitting room in which Hughes had had his dream, I'd moved to a bigger, lighter place, all of fifty yards away. But I now feel closer to its origins, and its presiding spirit or spirits. My new study is home to a collection of Hughes's work, including a manuscript of 'The Thought-Fox'; it also contains some of his fishing tackle, the apparatus by which he kept capturing creatures alive. The Pem Soc still meets there, now attracting student poets from across the University. I generally leave them to it (and the name is theirs – it really should be renamed for Ted): but last year, and again this, Peter Carpenter, himself a Pembroke graduate, returned to give two inspiring poetry workshops, when words flowed from my pen as well as everyone else's there with a speed and spontaneity and excitement at resources suddenly undammed in ways that made the room even more like Hughes' country than it already does. Not the Arvon's five days of total immersion, but a brief and bracing plunge, into close reading of fine new poems, close encounters with the inner life, that real life of language and of literature that Hughes never lost a chance to promote.

For the last four years, Pembroke has also been hosting as many readings as I can find room for, and Masterclasses run by the National Academy of Writing's director, the novelist (and yet another Pembroke English graduate) Richard Beard. For an hour he performs a public edit – constructive, energizing, clear-eyed practical criticism, always informed by supportive coaching – of two submissions of students' narrative prose. For the next hour, one of the Academy's patrons or another leading practitioner – to date, Kazuo Ishiguro, Frances Fyfield, Ian Marchant, Kevin Barry, Evie Wyld, Deirdre Madden, Alan Hollinghurst, Deborah Levy, amongst this list at least two graduates and one teacher of prestigious university creative courses – talks about his or her writing methods. Students and academics flock to these masterclasses from across Cambridge; there is a real hunger for them.

As a University, Cambridge has only recently begun to offer Creative Writing courses of its own, via its Institute for Continuing Education: as an internal examiner appointed by the English Faculty, I know how rapid the progress made by these developing writers can be, but I'm also aware, still, of the separation, often as real as it is perceived, between our two disciplines, despite the lecturing platforms and residencies the University and its colleges offer to writers, despite the prizes Cambridge offers for creative writing, at both Parts of the English Tripos, and the annual prize for a poem on a sacred subject. Perhaps because the city's other fine university, Anglia Ruskin, now does offer full undergraduate and postgraduate Creative Writing courses, my sense is that the gap won't, and perhaps shouldn't, close soon. But in the meantime, the magical hours when readers come together to write, and listen to writers reading, in rooms that feel suddenly larger for the encounter, give me real hope.

71

Peter Carpenter

Creative Writing: 'Moments of Extension'

' *banish the fears learnt early on* ' Julia Casterton

'*Fair seed-time had my soul*' Wordsworth

This essay is a personal account of what Creative Writing (from the times before I knew it as such) has meant to me as learner, teacher, writer, editor and publisher. I have written other essays and articles[1] that consider such roles in a more public, systematic way, so forgive digressions and liberties taken. To put you in the picture: I have been a teacher of English in secondary education since 1980, and have worked for university departments, notably posts at Reading and Warwick; I take students on residential courses, Arvon (where I have subsequently tutored and read) and at Ty Newydd, and have done so since 1994; each week I run writing workshops for students; I do outreach work for many organisations, in age ranging down to primary school groups. I co-direct a small press; I review and write critical essays, almost exclusively on poetry. So, I believe in the project: a man dabbles in verses and finds they are his life.

It is impossible to trace a steady course that tells you where things start.[2] However, it might best be shown by a moment in the autumn of 2010. I am clearing my late mother's house, going through the drawers of a bed-side cabinet, and I find a poem (with illustration) about an otter. The hand-writing is mine, at the age of around seven, I'd guess; I had never seen an otter first hand, I know this, but I had read Henry Williamson's *Tarka the Otter*. The scrap has survived. The adult self brings to it the reflex: 'Black is the wet otter's head, lifted': a line from Hughes in my head, a line from that survivor's manual, *Crow*. This moment brings me to a series of simple reflections: our teachers, often our best teachers, at whatever stage, are books, what we read; there are encouragements or 'provocations' or 'prompts' that lie hidden in our memory, that will outfox and possibly outlive our waking selves, the selves of the unreal 'real world' that we inhabit, the world of key-board tapping, online experience, Instagram.

I go along with Lowell when he pronounces ruefully at a reading,

---

[1] Most recently a long essay, 'Singing Schools and Beyond', that became Chapter Seventeen of *The Handbook of Contemporary British and Irish Poetry* (OUP, 2013) ed. Peter Robinson

[2] Heaney's account of where things started for him ('Mossbawn') is incomparable, a must-read; I came across it in *Worlds,* that life-bringing anthology of contemporary poets and poems, edited by Geoffrey Summerfield, in 1974.

'memory is genius'. How many starting points at subsequent workshops have been to 'raid' the memory? From a Joe Brainard 'I Remember' peg to hang some hats on, or a take on Peter Sansom's poem 'That was the day it snowed'? And how the life-histories, those mysterious and fractured, powerful and hidden narratives then spill out: The seeds are inside the apple/The apple is inside the seed (Lyubomir Nikolov). A further reflection: how then will future generations of would-be poets cope without the nurture of reading: meaning that protracted, intense, solitary activity, the immeasurable deepening and broadening of a world view that has nothing to do with the instant and everything to do with internalised conversations. This seems to run counter to the instant fix of google, copy and paste: the new virtual world of instant access and stimulus, images 'viral' in seconds, snapchat a running commentary on many lives. And educational agendas dealing with digital creativity, forgetting human creativity; government policy obsessed with mensuration, targets and testing. This world is too much with us. Or is it just my imagination, running away with me?

At secondary school Miss Jackson made us learn and write out great chunks of 'The Ancient Mariner'; Mr ('Sam') Sanders made us learn and write out poems by Tennyson and speeches from *Macbeth*. We groaned, but the process was for me life-changing, life-enhancing. I still have that material there, along with the plays and texts we studied at A Level, especially *King Lear*, Blake, Webster, Chaucer, and gobbets, for unseens as part of Cambridge preparation in keeping with Mr. Kenneth Curtis's Leavisite education. Spenser's portrayal of Gluttony, Chaucer's Temple of Mars, and Keats' 'She dwells with beauty; beauty that must die', all on one page. Studying these intense moments, internalising them, made me realise the power of language to preserve and extend, to allow a summoning from the past.

And connecting with a great teacher, as Kenneth Curtis was, in the sixth form, was the pivotal experience that allowed me to start to make sense of the world through poetry, with serious discussion of Wordsworth, Keats, Donne, Herbert, Shakespeare. And then to realise, as librarian, that a book of poems by Geoffrey Hill (I had no idea who he was) was dedicated to 'Kenneth Curtis'.[3] The book, the experience, the chance: I am indebted. I

---

[3] "9.9.42 Hill, Geoffrey W.", *Agenda*, 30.1-2, 1992, p. 122.

am still in conversation with all those elements.[4]

A reflection: methods of teaching and materials available were often primitive, but they allowed and made necessary what is now prized as 'independent' learning. I currently teach in a classroom with a smart-board and instant access to a world, almost any world, on a screen. My colleagues often carefully now choose poems for discussion, 'unseens', that have no on-screen baggage, no 'bite-size' guides. I think that education is a long game, for life, not just for Christmas: I liked that idea of 'growth' through English. Now it is too often encouraged to be no more than a fly-past ceremony via SparkNotes.

To Cambridge in 1976: there is no 'official' part of the Tripos that permits or encourages 'creative' work; there is an option to submit a portfolio of creative work at the end of one's Part Two, but this does not count towards the degree. The example of Ted Hughes at Pembroke and beyond shows how poetry flourished at the margins, was counter-culture, and against the grain.[5] The Arvon Foundation has its roots here: the feeling that the mainstream academic system was allowing no space to, or 'mowing down', its greatest minds. Nowhere in this process was there a workshop, a moment when the 'hearse' could be 'bump-started' to paraphrase Kit Wright. Weekly supervisions and essays, scholarship, dissertations, but no time or space set aside, even by practising writers, to spur others to write. What was at work seemed to be a continuation of a fear factor that had taken grip. Being 'creative' is informed by failure: 'and every attempt/Is a wholly new start, and a different kind of failure' (Eliot). The real failure was in a system that did not encourage and set in motion opportunities to allow those studying literature to become practitioners, to adapt some 'apprentice-master' relationship along the lines of American Creative Writing schools. It is thrilling that so many universities now embrace Creative Writing, offer it as something to study, although I have some caveats that I will voice later on.

---

[4] I have written about this at more length in the collection: *King Log* for *The North*, 2009: 'How important true teachers really are... the ones who live their subject. I was very lucky in this respect, because that year I met the real thing: Kenneth Curtis, my English teacher and form tutor. Tall, slightly austere, a rhythmic fair-haired moustache, Wordsworthian: he walked home some days up to Epsom Downs, eschewing the 406 bus up the hill. He seemed to understand, he spoke and read with dignity, weight and passion: he established with me true rapport. 'Thou art the thing itself.' I can see him again propelling the book my way from across his librarian's desk. Olive green cover. Ken's soft voice, offhand, a voice apparently not looking up from its marking: 'Try this. Come back and tell me what you make of it.'

[5] The Arvon Foundation has its roots here: Hughes' foreword to *The Way to Write* by John Fairfax and John Moat, xi –xix, 1981, is essential reading.

Reflection: how does a 'successful' Creative Writing culture come about? There is no simple button to click. It is no surprise, following the feeding-frenzy of preparation and assessment for exams at the ages of (at least) 11, 13, 16, 18, the drilled instructions and inherited wisdoms concerning 'past papers', that many students enter and then leave their secondary education either jaded or anxious when they are asked to pen to paper, to be 'creative.' They've got this far and they don't want to 'get it wrong'. As Mary Kinzie points out, reading is like writing 'in beginning in uncertainty and driving towards speculation and experiment.' Such a drive towards 'speculation and experiment' needs a kick-start. Demons have to be driven away: what better than the democratic vulnerability of a writing group outside classes or supervisions, where all involved take a chance to begin afresh?

I am speaking as a convert. In 1993 I went on an Arvon Foundation Writing Course at Totleigh Barton, Devon. I had continued to write poetry after university and through hectic teaching schedules, but had lost confidence in it, side-lined it, however much it nagged. I had been a teacher for thirteen years, but nothing prepared me for the initial terror and buzz of reading out in front of the group, of showing work to the two tutors, or the rush of being liberated by a week (a whole week!) of writing workshops and reading and talk. It was a community of feeling: this was what I wanted to do and where I felt I belonged. I had to know one thing: to continue, or forget it. The tutors allowed me to continue, gave me a well-managed 'yes, but...' It was a start. To learn technique, not mannerisms, came next. The hard bit was to keep on keeping on, as Bob Dylan puts it. Thus followed years of shaping work, immersing myself in reading, allowing material to gestate, rejecting most of it, then sending a tiny percentage of the poems out. It was, though, that initial 'jump-start' that gave me permission to breathe, and thus the need to share the experience. In 1994 we took students on the first of now annual trips to Devon with a group of raw, wannabe writers; the work they produced astonished us, and them. Our tutors were Alan Brownjohn and the late Michael Baldwin; our guest reader was Ted Hughes, telling the students very firmly never to study English at university. Over 300 students from the school have now had this experience. Our Arvon anthology one year had this as part of an editorial: 'Arvon is unique. It sounds clichéd, doesn't it? However, it is far removed from any cynicism. It is fair to say that getting over a dozen teenage boys to happily inhabit a place with no TV, on internet or even mobile phone signal is no mean feat.'

One of the things the students learnt then was resilience via a truth: no work arrives perfectly formed at the first shot. (Ginsberg may have it 'first thought, best thought', but look at the drafts of 'Howl'.) Far better to value what Ann La Motte (in her invaluable 'Bird by Bird') terms 'the shitty first draft'. Thus other educational bonuses: learning to take advice, to collaborate, to draft work, to persevere. The drafting involved is not for assessment, another mark for GCSE or A Level coursework or for a higher education module. Samuel Beckett has it: 'Ever tried. Ever failed. No matter. Try again. Fail again. Fail better.' There is great scepticism about the nature of workshops. They can go wrong, the group dynamic can affect things; there can be a 'group wrecker' as Alan Brownjohn put it. And poetry cannot be 'willed'[6] into being; there is no guarantee of 'production'.

Here are some of my own ground rules: the group has to be voluntary, but all are welcome. All have to write, including the workshop leaders; there will be chances to share work, but it does not have to be read out. Sometimes workshops are led by the students themselves. Respect all work produced (in the security of a 'what goes on tour, stays on tour' atmosphere) and 'don't worry' if things don't work out.[7] What happens in a workshop? Simple: all write. Exercises, writing games, usually opening with some 'free writing' (writing at speed without stopping for a couple of minutes, sometimes with a prompt such as 'I opened the door and...'). Try it. Don't stop. Other elements might require visual or aural prompts, very often exemplary models from other writers. We all become beginners again: you have to be vulnerable. Barriers (fear or scepticism) break down. We share the word-hoard. Another thing: keep a notebook. Jot down, value, go back to first efforts. It's serious play. Fun.

David Morley takes it one stage further: 'Writing creatively can feel a little like working out logistical, even mathematical, challenges. Writing Games provide this elegant calculus in taut form. A bare page can terrify; a game simulates the real thing; or is a means of keeping your hand in, like playing scales. With practice, simulations can become the real thing. No writer creates a book at one sitting; they write it in stages...each stage requires several drafts. Writing games clone this process.'

The impact of Creative Writing classes can be stunning. Outsiders wonder what people actually write about. One answer comes in the form of a metaphor. A writer learns to burgle his/her own house: a good workshop will allow students to subdue the guard dog of their own scepticism to enter the house, to raid what has always been there (the word-hoards,

---

[6] Shelley's words from his *Defence of Poetry* (1821): 'Poetry is not like reasoning, a power to be exerted according to the determination of the will. A man cannot say, "I will compose poetry." The greatest poet even cannot say it; for the mind in creation is as a fading coal, which some invisible influence, like an inconstant wind, awakens to transitory brightness...'

[7] Ann Sansom: 'it is not a competition; no one is reading this... You can't do it wrong' as reported in *Lifesaving Poems* edited by Anthony Wilson, Bloodaxe, 2015, p.25, and heard and echoed with variants by the current writer.

the memory troves, the stories). A connected art is to find ways of saying it: as Robert Frost put it: 'all the fun is in how you say a thing'. Form is meaning: what might be seen as initial restraints (in form or time) very often liberate. A time limit provides pressure but removes anxiety: no one is expected to produce a great work in a couple of minutes, but often, for this very reason, the germ of something special emerges. (Peter Sansom gave a young Simon Armitage key advice: to find the material, change the lens.) To write poems, you need to read them. Workshops are sustained by models of 'good practice' that range from Anglo Saxon kennings to Benjamin Zephaniah's 'Body Talk'. Creative writing is creative reading: imitation and influence are allies.

Why and how then should such singing schools thrive and matter? Why? First, we have a duty towards all those in education to resist bad technique and bad faith in our language, to work away from the easy plunder of sensationalist or fake or formulaic writing. Second, to realise that writing at its best is fun and a matter of liberation, not drudgery, some form of trial: 'It's wonderful, there's nothing else like it, you write in a trance. You can be sitting there but inwardly dancing... you're full alive.' (Les Murray)

How? Teachers of literature have to get their hands dirty, to follow their own instructions, to have a go at a sonnet or a villanelle or some free verse, to read 'from the inside'. They may also develop the knack (the poet Director of Creative Writing at the University of Exeter, Andy Brown is brilliant at this) of sniffing out poems as source material for writing, not just for commentary work and study. However, Creative Writing classes are the natural home for those who want alternatives from a set of orthodoxies. I have ongoing first-hand experience to tell me that all students can be taught to become better writers, but not that they can be put on some production line of instruction to become writers *per se*. Universities face some very difficult choices over the coming years and the humanities are under increasing pressure to 'give value for money'.

Those teaching Creative Writing are under increasing pressure to measure 'outcome', to regulate the muse. Technique needs to be taught, but it may be informed by an adverse reaction to certain models, including those chosen by those running such courses. Sessions on how to win an Eric Gregory Award, for example, are laudable, yet somehow worry me a little, hinting at a culture of corporate upward mobility. Some poets setting out are desperate to be published quickly, or to write to please the editor of a particular magazine or journal, or to try to will the poem out, to write to order. Editors have a duty to be more than just nodding dogs on the back-seat of the car. The first duty of the writer is to the intractable material they work with, language. To allow themselves to be surprised, to be prepared to start all over, to battle. Heaney registers perfectly the precariousness and irrationality of the whole process: 'You survive in your own esteem not by the corroboration of theory but by the trust in certain moments of satisfaction which you know intuitively to be moments of extension. You are confirmed by the visitation of the last poem and threatened by the elusiveness of the next one'.[8]

---

[8] From 'Feeling into Words', *Preoccupations*, Faber, 1980, p.54.

Zoë Brigley Thompson

A Note on 'Learning' Creative Writing

The value of Creative Writing courses has been hotly debated in recent years, one notorious case being the proclamation by Hanif Kureishi that such study at university level is a waste of time. What is not so often quoted, however, is Kureishi's comment on the equality of expression fostered in Creative Writing classes: 'What's more important with creative writing is that everybody gets to speak.' [1]

Kureishi might be commenting negatively about the therapeutic potential of writing, and yet there is something else here, perhaps the sense that Creative Writing has the potential to aid students in fostering certain attitudes of mind that, in general, might be beneficial for themselves and others. Creative Writing is after all about imagination, and imagination is key to human understanding and human progress. Writing poetry need not be solipsistic or indulgent. It is instead about creating what Dennis Sumara defines as 'interpreted bridges between what is held in memory, what currently exists, and what is predicted about the future' and such 'imagining is central to human cognition.' [2] Imagination is also what combats human failings. Ignorance, doubt, fear, misunderstanding: all fall away in the face of an empathetic, imaginative outlook.

It is worth noting too that the act of imagining is not the privilege of a particular class or group. You do not have to have studied at an elite university to write poetry. You do not necessarily need a great deal of money, though you do need time (something that is not always easy) and space: a room of one's own as Virginia Woolf puts it. Creative Writing courses can give writers the space and time necessary to finish their work, though that relies of course on having the funds to pay.

Creative Writing courses can also aid writers in other ways, however. What you need as a writer is to be an observer. Discussing Creative Writing and education, Sumara suggests that 'Deep insight emerges from the hard work of interpreting one's relations with people, to objects people have

---

[1] Qtd. in Alice Jones and Nick Clark, 'The Independent Bath Literature Festival: Creative Writing Courses are a Waste of Time...' *The Independent*, 4th March, 2014. Access online: <http://www.independent.co.uk/arts-entertainment/books/news/the-independent-bath-literature-festival-creative-writing-courses-are-a-waste-of-time-says-hanif-9166697.html>.

[2] Dennis Sumara, *Why Reading Literature in Schools Still Matters: Imagination, Interpretation, Insight* (Mahwah, N.J.: L. Erlbaum, 2002), p. 5.

made (including narratives that describe and explain experience), and to the more-than-human world'.[3] To reach such insights, the poet must cultivate a state of mind that is curious and open to new experiences. This means withholding judgment and looking at things from a number of different angles. Sumara concludes that the 'deep insight' that characterizes successful poetry 'is usually surprising, occurring unexpectedly, emerging from curious places.'[4] A Creative Writing course cannot magically conjure this quality, but it can certainly encourage certain habits of mind that might be productive.

[3] Sumara, p. 5.
[4] Ibid

Omar Sabbagh

The Cedar Never Dies

My country, my love,
Let me speak to you now in a foreign tongue,
Quipping against the flaming madness
Now begun,
The language in which I body my caress,
My missive in Dove...

My country, my love,
Tell them the Cedar never dies, and She will rise,
A Phoenix without the need
Of ligaments or knees...
A sour privilege to be, and concede
Against the flung velvet of a glove

The asking seed of daring gauntlets, my
Country, my love:
Let these words meet, though in a different tongue,
Your flesh of green, your never-ending rungs.

Prayer

For more than a decade, the wick has thrived.
I've lit candles for my youth, the untarnished.
Now and again, the flame has swerved,
Following slim whispers of a wind. My nerves
Have been like sprinters, harried at the finish
By countless breaths, by numbers' hives
Buzzing like harridans through heart, lungs.
And I know, after all, the body survives.
And I know the tail that slithers after song –
The beast, the beast after the music. Wrong,
Yes: I've many to my name, hanged by knives
Of fame, a decade and more. I live by the gift
Of knowing grief, battling it, lifting it into life.
I've often wondered, Lord. I've often wondered.

Peace As We May Find It

The gnarl-lipped monster growls: that he is our total!
Beware of his Being; Being: the daft, outright denier
Of the awful circumstance (round as it is tight)
May be to be the place a paltry midget finds

Flight from his erstwhile shortness, un-preferred
In a bad world's grime: System of prongs and System of signs
Mastering all / telling all but the True – that feather
Of a light touch – *The Man*: and a Mind behind the *Rôle* ...

*

Thoughts to solve (to salve) the wounds of a speared nation
May be just so: pyres to the old dogmas / the back-bent Organs
Where insects strive – thinking like lions – for deep Foundations ...

We've to be practical, more than pure: a moving arrow for
A moving target... Let the 'clout' and the 'kudos' stir
As much as they will: our weapons will shimmy like the world:

To concur with Time's rhapsody / that fast that secular chill
Freezing all to still the hot ideals: of even the bravest wills...
True: Love's a poem that Lebanon killed. (*But Lebanon lives...*

Ben Parker

Fallow

for C&D

How is it that the evening you told me
about the large deer you missed
and the smaller one that you hit
another two appeared for you
later that night like wayside mourners?

A deer to me is a distant thing:
not just the car's shell, but fences,
woodland and darkness separate
our ways of being. Whereas you
by having once suddenly impinged

on the world of hoof and horned brow
are now inescapably a part of it.
The hot breath you watched expire
by moonlight left its acid scent
on your hair and clothes. You became

a factor in their reckoning, and they
in yours. Two paths running parallel
have crossed just once and even if
the travellers never meet again
they know the signs, can read the tracks.

Metastasis

Not as you had supposed
from the Latin 'beyond stillness'
but from the Greek
for 'change'.
Its very origin as hard to pin down
as the disease itself.
Instead of that familiar speech
of ancient Italy
we have been tricked
by a language
where the very alphabet is strange.
It is on your tongue now.
It has begun to move.

Joseph Rennie

That's Not Him

I lost my father to a lie he told himself in church.
I lost him on frosted windows.
Lost him as our mother once lost us
to the night.

When I think about these things.
When I see him in pictures,
I see a face with no teeth;
they are gone now spat out in my
dreams.
I see His ears large tuned to god.

His angry shouts have turned to praise.
His children turned to adults.
In his mind I am still the boy he made laugh
as my head was stitched.

He has learnt how to build his church.
He feeds the rice hungry religion.
He has been a father to them.

I have a story I tell myself.
I lost my father to a lie he told himself in church.
I lost him like you would a tooth.
He fell out of the mouth of my world.

Bernadette McCarthy

Modern Conversational Arabic

'He is a brother not a father.' Serving
the girls leaf-tea from her thermos,
my Arabic teacher talked about her husband
who was courting high court caliphs
into signing refugees' papers, stringing

their tales from one night to the next.
'A good man.' And without him, syntax snagged,
though between us the ragged ends met:
her bride-price mucking up the Nile callows,
an equation that outwore the cloven years

of asylum; the ministerial handshake,
ached for, yet awkward in the end,
cuffs brushing at a wake. She kittered
an empty cup from my hand, snapped her veil:
'I'm sorry for the troubles in the East,'

then took the scrap of chalk again
and pulling back her sleeve blazed us down
the seams of sound succeeding sound, tonguing
tacit vowels into the chastity
of consonants; as algebra binds

the broken parts she wove a universe
into her lace of ligature. '*Assalumu alaikum.*'
I knew that the words were backwards,
that a dagger hung over the aliph,
an assassin could stop my glottis

with the sadist twist of *Ṣād*,
but followed the letters off the page
into her eyes; Donyazad, world-freer,
on the azimuth of her brow, who with
the wisdom of a scripture seemed to say:

'You can burn me but the words will still be spoken;
you can shoot me but my children will live on;
you can scorn me but I am your mother, your daughter,
your father and your brother.'

Rachel Plummer

A God Between the Sheets

I found him muddled in the crepe paper
bandages of my bed sheets. About a foot tall,
a little bearded china doll. I knew at once
he was a god. He had that look about him –
self-important, mind on other things.

Jehova, I called him. *Freyr. Vishnu.*

He blinked in metal stages.
His voice was plated tin.
I let him share my pillow, his tiny head
beside mine like a child's, his greedy golden
hands hogging all the covers.

Fagus, Buxenus, Robor, I sighed in my sleep

and dreamed of gold leaf trees
winding their light through my bedroom
window, sinking their heavy, precious roots
through the white soil of my mattress,
each bud a goldfish or starfish or herring.

I starred my fingers on the pillow. *Allah. Allah.*

He was not gone by daylight. He pinched
me awake with porcelain fingers.
For breakfast a burnt offering – toast in bed
and the last scrape of butter from the dish.
It oiled his jutting chin, shining his beard.

Baldr?

I thought I heard the clank of his eyes
rolling sarcastically back in their sockets.
I wanted to put him on the mantelpiece
a delicate figurine among the photographs.
I wanted to pose him in a glass bell jar.

Ishvara, I said. *Don't you have places to be?*

But he clung to my bedsheets fiercely
and was still there when I got back
from work that night, mummified in duvet.
Surely, I thought, my bed is no place
for a god.

Orcus. I pointed to the television. *Abassi. Look at this.*

I showed him the geography channel.
The wide spaces of Earth, the lips
of impact craters; salt flats and cities,
the Gobi desert and the Mariana Trench.
I showed him rainforest.

You would rust here, Hephaestus.

I showed him a photograph of the Earth
from space, a bubble suspended
in the galaxy's amber. I showed him
the universe, which stretches itself
to encompass all that is within its membrane.

This is the Alpha and Omega, I told him.

He turned away, his miniature face blank
as marble. So I switched to the news,
which was bloody and flinching as ever.
The flickering screen cut a path through my ribs.
Suffering, I said. *This is suffering.*

If you have power to help these people, Hachiman...

When I looked back, I saw him already sleeping.
He is still there now, small and silver
on the goose down. He never leaves my bed.
His soft breath rattles like prayer beads
from my window. I lie awake at night and name him

Svarog. Jade Emperor. Jarri. Yahweh. Elohim.

Charlotte Eichler

At the Cathedral of the Spilled Blood

We buy eggs painted with the silence of snow,
scarves wrapped tight around our mouths –

ice crystals prickle our noses when we breathe.
Men hiss   *devushki*   from car windows

saying 'sing for us'   and later
'of course you can sing, a pretty girl like you' –

more voices from the crawling Porsche
and a bear-huge man on the path.

She's matryoshka small in her fur-lined hood
and mute as a doll.

Note:
devushki: girls in Russian
matryoshka: Russian nesting doll

Sarah Sibley

Crawlers Lane

In the moonlight the newly tarmacked lane
is a stretch of grey goosebumps.
You're exposed to open fields,
but there's no wind, and in this calm,
once you're half way down,
and too far from the nearest house,
you'll see an apparition of the Howe Wood witch;
her baby made of straw disintegrating
until she holds nothing.
She will look for it until dawn:
outside your bedroom window
or in the churchyard, where disturbed villagers
fall back to sleep hugging their knees.
Once, at the end of the lane,
the hardest man in the village
cracked open with grief –
field mice crawled inside him;
at the end of the lane, impaled on railings,
a polystyrene burger box, mouth open,
laughed and laughed.

School Pool Patsies

Prune-fingered and blue
from June to late August.
In the changing rooms
we attack our swimming caps
for heads shuttlecock smooth,
then do a chain-gang stomp
through verruca dip,
dive in after a hoop or a brick.
Us girls shy Lycrad gazelles
to their boy blaze:
hollering and dive bombing.
We go out in a talcum haze,
run red eyed to cold classrooms;
ponytails dripping, shirts
sticking to our backs,
boys' bellies smarting.

The Outer Limits

From the books that wash up on the tide,
we learn about the outside world.
At night we bury our jewellery boxes in the salt flats,
hoping the songs drift beyond
to the outer limits.
Our older sisters are the first to leave.
They go drifting into the night:
our bright and lovely satellites.
Looking out from portholes to a threatening sky,
their dreams roll one way across the deck
then collapse on themselves.
What would they find out there?

Katelyn VerSprill

Lapse

i

It was still light at nine that night.
There was a cup floating in the garden pond.
Aunt Laura and Dave were milling around, picking
at the remaining food and drinking the last wine.
My brother and I were wiping down the patio
when we heard the muffled shouting:
bitch and *whore* coming through the glass door.
I looked inside just in time to see the slap
and Mom hitting her head off the floor.

ii

It was around nine or ten that night.
There was a cup floating in the garden pond.
Laura and Dave had left minutes before
and the lawn was littered with crisps, empty cups.
We were cleaning the patio furniture
when we heard the stifled shouting:
I didn't and *that's not true* seeping
through the glass door. I looked inside just
in time to see the slap, Mom falling to the floor.

iii

It was late that night, maybe after ten.
There was a cup in the pond.
I'm not sure who was still around
from the party, but there was so much mess.
My brother and I were cleaning the patio
when we heard them shouting: *bitch*,
and *that's not true* from the kitchen.
I looked inside in time to see the slap
and Mom stumbling backward to the wall.

iv

I'm not sure what time it was but
it was still light and there was a cup
in the pond. I have no idea who
was still around, but my brother and I
were cleaning the patio when we heard
the shouts: *bitch*, *whore*, *that's not true*.
I looked through the glass door into the kitchen,
saw the slap and turned away before
I could see anything more.

Siân Thomas

Hindleap, Ashdown Forest, 22nd January

A day as grey as a sieve that's caught
moss-felted trees, inevitable mud
and the rags of rooks' nests.

We used to come here all the time
when I was a kid. We had picnics
and spotted the place with dalmatians
who stole our sandwiches and rolled in fox.

Now the colours have faded.
Winter storms have spread branches.
The floor is a miniature forest: twigs
stick up and I'm a giant, squelching through.

I'm an adult. I follow path rivers, down
till I reach the valley and the small stream
that's almost clear but orange-bottomed
chalybeate, like it's fed by rusty pipes.

I've no clue where I am (often the way:
I leave the car park, full of confidence,
with all my grown up nonchalance,
till I reach the place that asks,
What if you never get back?).

I sit on the stream's side, in cold
January leaves and write about loss.
Water flits beneath the bridge.

There's a sieve's worth of sunlight
and the trees are dripping, but
the path's turn is mine too –

and the birds know who I am:
I'm the mouth of the stream.
The stream stands up, climbs the hill.

Duddleswell, Ashdown Forest, 27ᵗʰ March

Rooks are my black jacket. The Downs rise, blue as ghosts,
a sky away in the never-end, the continuum of cold.
To them I must look like an exclamation mark, like a crow's
yell. I'm the black in spring's blue haze, the cold thing,

breathing birdsong. Rowan leaves leap at a magpie and the voices
of other birds come bearing down the mud of the ride.
This spring has gorse teeth. I'm with it, brisk as the first-born bee,
as the rooks, my punctuation mates, my flappers and divers,

my absolutes, though I'm alone. As the sun eases over, squints
my cheeks, down I go, to poke about in the woods and snuffle
like the crow I am. I'll unzip my feathers and sniff the wrinkled
oaks, where the ground's as black as my eye.

Gary Matthewman

Mitsuko

With eager grace and spirited poise
she flits and darts across the void
to this slab of oil-slicked walnut shadow
and shimmering ivory perch. Here,
with nodded thanks, blinking through applause,
she settles. Folds her wings. Begins.

Unwinding her sparrowhawk mind, so she flies
high above barlines, dampers, strings – spins
an exquisite yarn, a hairline twine, splintering
the air with porcelain cries. On each phrase
a milk-fine glaze that speaks of rococo pride.

Followers of this woman of the cloth, we her flock are
carried along as pinpoint turn unfurls
and recapitulation tilts her rolling pearls
homeward. Reaching the altar – little and plain –
she lays down her peaceful, sleeping prey:
        this final chord.

Head still bowed, she draws up her hands into cut-glass
silence, and unveils an eighteenth-century cloud.

Note on Mitsuko Uchida:
Japanese concert pianist, is for many the 'High Priestess of Mozart', and her playing
is known for its crystalline clarity, delicate precision of attack, bell-like tone and
fearsome intelligence. She is rather bird-like in the way she moves at the piano.

Tess Jolly

Owl

In a corridor leading between carrels and tuck-shop
    I beat my wings. The bell lamented another hour
in the lives of girls marching: the kohl-lashed redhead
    whose rat nibbled a frill at her breast where she warmed it,
the packs of sixth-formers whose hidden blades
    would make you smile, then grin from ear to ear
if you breathed *a word*. The ghost of the girl
    who dipped shining nibs in the inkwells of her eyes.

Fledgling-soft, I flew through familiar rooms
    where bandy legs stuck from beneath the desks
like middle fingers, and old taunts fluttered in my heart.
    Remembering me as someone she'd taught
in a school in a distant location, Miss Barker
    ummed and *ahhed,* asked if there was *anything she could do?*
I lied and made a nest between the lines I had to write,
    my song striving against the white cliffs of my bones.

At night, all in the dorm asleep, I perched at the open window,
    felt the forest's sweet flesh roil beneath my claws.
Knowing then the freedom to move silent and terrible,
    the instinct to slip breath from a body
like fruit from its shell, I swooped - a feathered angel
    crossing earth. Far from the tethering stalks and roots
I shaped my beak to the moon's slick curve, pressed
    the rags of my words like fur to the tip of my tongue.

Swim, they said

so you swam, oh how you swam
and the water made a drowned city
of the house where you'd played knock-down ginger,
the White Horse sign swaying in the tide.
Dead-Man's Alley lashed like a sea-dragon
from the dark end of the cul-de-sac, encrusted
with fragments of the tea-set you found in the air-raid shelter,
the glistening pear drops you said were nail varnish
when your parents came upstairs to ask.
Those letters you almost left beneath your sister's pillow
were translucent as jellyfish, the ink drained away.
Swim further they said so you swam, you swam
as if your life depended on it, between the bones
of bike sheds rusted to wrecks, the stumps of trees
that sheltered you that summer after the exams,
when Sultana could no longer run to the playing fields
and suck water from bottles frozen overnight,
when you saw her walk each day towards
a man waiting in a car. After they drove away
there was only your mother hurrying up the drive,
her hair tied in a scarf, soil on her knees and hands.
She should have come an hour ago but now
you've vanished, the gates are locked, even your neighbour
has hung his last bag of sweets over the fence and gone inside.
Swim deeper they said so you swam.

With My Hand in His Pocket

I will thread his shirt-button onto the laces
    of a long-distance runner, that his heart
might beat on the moors like the moon's bright palm,
    that he might clothe the soil in the fabric
of half-light, fasten night and day together.

I will wind his house-key in the satin ribbon
    of a ballet dancer's shoe, that his skin
might remember touch and its absence
    as she pirouettes and turns, that the earth
might yield again to his footsteps' passing.

I will press each bright boiled sweet
    onto a walking boot's tongue, that the wind
might blow across the tarn of his mind
    and his stories rise again – whispering
in the cotton-grass, echoed from cairn to cairn.

I will lodge his loose change in the sole
    of a farmer's Wellington boot. On his knees
in the garden as if rooting for head or hoof,
    he'll whistle the old songs of copper and silver
to draw out the wildflowers, the difficult bones.

Though he is broken by what he has tried to break
    and cannot break, though his thoughts
are crushed glass and his fingers have become
    strange featherless birds fluttering
from the branches of his lap, pecking empty air –

I will remember his hand closing around
    my small hand, and as our shadows lengthen
in the dying light, I will whisper love's prayer.

Georgina Pett-Ridge

Leaves

I threw them as if
the trees had shed again.
You watched. They
spread up after the arc
of my hand, following my denial of
physics, folding over themselves in no
order, until gravity pawed at their
sides. They swung
back with the air, tipping
themselves up,
down,
all around,
in the dying colours of autumn.
But I did not see them – stepping
back – only your heavy
fist, and the red flecks down my shirt.

Caroline Clark

Beautiful Loss

Over in un-
cut autumn
light all before
and possible
pouring in

there in golden
so fleeting
settled peace
comes to a place
passed

unnatural I may
be this is magnified
life   I
follow for but seconds

its scent on
me all life-
long   looking
and losing
looking and losing.

Tessa Foley

Older

You wished to be her father, hold her downy arms
And guide them whilst her eyes are closed, she could make
A fairy cake or finger paint on walls with a whisper on to
Her shirted shoulder, it was your shirt as swaddling,
You closed her in to cotton cossets when she sat breathless
And uncovered on top of the duvet, staring to the east window.

She waited in the bed for you, a goodish girl and wished
She was your daughter, on the seesaw so you'd see her silhouette
Against the sun, risen and felled, proud to watch her hair bounce
As restless water, she lived in your house when you asked her,
Lay in your shadow from a tiny lamp, listening to a page a night,
Before practice simplified itself and you did as was expected.

Nine times out of ninety, the bed was unprotective, less than ideal
For you or the unready maid so, best to blow straight through
And hold all out to hold her for nine whole hours, in the dark,
Under the duvet, while she scratched at her finer skin and in the morning,
You only felt the toast crumbs between you and the sheets once she'd
Gone downstairs, barefoot and sunlit and you shook your smiling head.

You were pleased to give her daisies from the park and delighted by
The petals landing on her face, if only she'd been really yours,
She couldn't be, not with those blue eyes that once belonged to him
Who excused himself at every birthday, when you hold hands,
You swing them, lift her under lampposts all-praying it won't end
Or that you're back to bed too often to make them understand.

Zoë Brigley-Thompson

The Hole in the Wall

I gave her what she asked: had she asked more
I would have given it.
                        – Walter Savage Landor, 'Pan and Pitys'

Like setting an eye to a hole in the wall,
he is thinking about her again, wondering
if it was wrong, assuring himself it was right.
He still has the photo he took when he tied
her to a chair. Like setting his eye to a crack
looking through at what happened, but she
cannot see him, doesn't know he is there.

He is dropping her off at her house on the hill
and follows her to the door, where she leans
for a minute before fumbling with the key.
Or that time when she sewed a button
on his shirt pulling the thread
through the eye, methodical and firm.

That was before it all began. He loved her
fifteen-year-old pleasure, how easy it was
to make her come, but he couldn't find his own
without hurting her. Like putting his eye to a gap,
he sees her again, but sometimes her face turns to him,
deliberate and wooden, and her eyes lance him.

Like the time in the pine forest – planted to replace
the trees that died – when she faced him under a moonless,
clouded evening, and at the edge of the frosted needles
were the brightly lit windows of a small brick house,
and he wanted to fuck her where the children might look
out of the window at any moment, wanted to fuck her
nastily like his fat father fucked his mother.

He could have been a nurse or a geologist,
could have cared for animals or the elderly.
He knows he is kind, compassionate by nature,
so years later, he writes, and the letters come
spidering from the email to tell her:
Sometimes I sit quietly and try to remember
on long boring drives or sometimes at work.
Barely a day goes by that I don't think of you.
He is still gazing as far as a continent
to snowy woods where he buries her waist deep.

Syringe

After James Merrill and John Ashbery

When he puts his mouth to her, he draws out
the scale of love and dread like a misted breath
from wet lips on an icy day, or exhausted
fog from the mouth of a smoker,
all tar and charred things and winter
crouched on the fire escape in the back alley.

So long since the summer at the marsh
when she stalked the boardwalk alone, the bees
and bluebottles so lazy they could not stop
colliding with her bare arms and shoulders,
their wings zipping and jolting,
each like a tiny electric shock.

She stood there watching for a long time,
the reeds and rushes spinning and bowing
like the white noise between TV channels,
dipping and rising like a waltz,
each thinking blade knowing the others,
every move with mathematical grace.

She is swallowing, gulping down pebbles
to rattle in the empty place inside;
a hollow needle longing to be full.
Like Syrinx, the reed-woman, she makes
herself long, spiked and narrow, speaking
only when the wind blows through her.

She wishes she had met her husband sooner;
perhaps at fifteen, him skinny and slight
before his growth spurt, running the lakeshore
alone, and her breastless, all hipbones and elbows,
spun back to what happened so long before the rape
in some small town, one indifferent summer.

Valerie Jack

Aspects of a Dreamboat

They drain the round pond in the public gardens
and find little silted boats, with the odd
flake of paint still clinging on to dreams of
fastest, best, most beautiful.
And you say yes, I had
    a submarine.
        a yacht.
            a battle ship.

    Self-painted shades of military grey.
    Man in his bubble ready to go down.

        Though father forbade toys,
        Granna taught an origami boat –
        symmetrical sail that switched
        into a tighter version of itself, and back out.

            Year long, with a cargo block
            you could take on and off,
            and guns you'd think slid forward to fire -
            best bits from different types of ship –
            carved and varnished by my father,
            who was Captain. I practised
            Gunboat Diplomacy ('blast the hell out of 'em')
            till fantasy outgrew the bath,
            house became ship propelled by
            washing machine, with me Chief Engineer,
            three purple ribbons on my raincoat,
            sitting alone at Captain's table.

The stream near Granna's garden
had water only sometimes,
even then my ships would run aground
and sag dissolving into mud.

I wished the bath was polar white not the
bohemian orange my parents chose
and that ponds were less brown.
What was the point
if I couldn't see the man?

Yet you say

>I never had
>a toy boat as a kid.
>it would have had
>a tall white sail with red and blue detail,
>and sailed with willow down
>over a green lake
>and we'd have been
>inseparable for a summer.

Patrick Widdess

Hollywood actress

Surprisingly, she's all you'd expect
sprawled on a limo in a thousand dollar dress.
Eyes hide behind shades
beating back LA's rays.
Hair blonde and wavy,
styled by Gehry.
Cigarette an extra slender finger
slowly turning to silky vapour.
Beyond Rolling Stones red lips,
a row of teeth huge, straight and white
as the letters H to D on the hillside.
Her smile is HD,
her laughter's in Dolby
ringing out from this dust-free, shadowless lay-by.
And when she blows you a kiss you want to hit rewind.

Love's organ

Not the heart,
asymmetrical lump of gristle,
but the lungs
intricately crafted bellows
to your flaming soul.
Steadily heaving, infusing
blood with scarlet passion,
feeding air through the throat's fragile machinery
voicing every word, sigh and song.
Bagpipes of Cupid, play on.

Matt Howard

Total Reconstruction of the Burned Face

'make a face which does not excite pity or horror.
By so doing we can restore a lost soul to normal living'.
Sir Archibald McIndoe

At all costs eyes must be kept from drying,
though streaming will need treatment in time.
Lids are too fragile, stitching them uncertain –
to blink freely cannot be understated.

Only then can we refigure the architecture
of a face, its harmony and balance,
so that the airman may blush into his skin
and smile with it, rather than beneath it.

Over decades each face will pass
under another's care; further exposure to light
brings contracture, new scars, need for running repairs

and of course we shall look, they are faces
disfigured in fire, but we must not stare:
we are trustees of each other.

The Chop Blonde

The Half Moon, Mildenhall 1943

A real smasher with film star eyes,
yet for her now there are no more dances,
no straight-backed blushing advances.

Though only one man ever set course for her bed,
six others were charted to follow.

She will sit and nurse her one port wine,
those eyes burning with the faces
of all her bomber boys past closing time.

Heather Wells

Strange

Intimacy lost
upon a wave
rippling out to sea
when once
it engulfed me.

Your form felt now
by another's hands
How firm you must now
feel to her.

Luke Palmer

Prognosis

The question sticks
like a plate boundary.
Continents of stone
around a narrow throat.
Voice box held by dumb weights
like an old clock
not wound up enough
in a day bright room
full of fleshy words
– gauze, swab –
the neutral
smell of latex.

Dust gathers.
Fills the mouth like a glacier.
Plucks the rocks
from the larynx
by the force of its compressed dust weight.
The question trickles out
in the melt dust
blindness.
Silent cataracts.
Dust storms. Dust burn
as cold as dust.
Dust freeze and dust thaw
weathers the fissures
the dust finds,
widens each slit
to an onslaught of pillowing dust.
Branches of dust and fluted dustfalls
unique formations
dust cathedrals, spires
vaulted halls of sepulchral dust
beneath the crevassed dust surface.

Vast shelves of dust
split and crack
collapsing in arcing trails
of fine dust crystals.
Growling from the dust belly of the earth
pulling itself along
and down.

Time does something.

The dust floes retreat

Dust
further each year.
Wide gulfs separate
the dust bergs.
Terrible, magnificent shapes appear
as they melt.

Pip Sequence – viii

We speak of you like keysmiths
all latch and tie and turn and tumble.
There are spoons rolled in yoghurt pots
many words to explain then place
on pictures, charts and sequences
to help us break your code. The series
of jagged contractions drawn
on a timeline is too easy for simile
and everything must be upright
and forward and open always
so that the pelvis will unlock and
you will announce your entry
a snotty sneeze from the cervix
after a period of engagement
and the placenta suite will unstitch
in watchmaker's precision
from the uteral wall.

But we are mostly told
what you already know –
that you will spin
into the world
unfasten everything
and leave us all revealed.

Lucy Ingrams

Sea-fishing

from
         the stern
   to the village
         shore, a dozen
metres, twenty-four
and we're changing –
                              stacked sand-still for yielding flex,
      sun-cream cloy for wind and brine;
      a kilometre – dogs, beach-balls, kids shrunk pennant-small,
                        more, and the harbour concentrate dilutes:
      our seeing thins and spreads, sifts relations
                        between freedoms… this throw of tides, the rides of sky.
         You navigate by haggard geometries of rock,
   cave-eyed bays and sea-crow shacks, while
                        in my shifting gravities of self, some pursed
      valves breach, a limpet marker
         slides. I anchor the fine
         gill nets the sea
   will cook tonight, and let
      our land wars
            drop – my salt
         heart drift
            again, near
               you

Lighter than air

Dare to be scared! See the fair
from the air! Acceleration flings
us to the trees. Gravitation hurls
us back again. *Dare to be scared!*
See the fair from the air!

Persons of a soft nature should watch
before they ride. Freddie's Revenge,
Body Rock, Stratosphere, Miami
Trip. *Persons of a soft nature*
should watch before they ride.

Acceleration flings us to the trees. Gravitation
hurls us back again. Inside the crammed
adrenaline, one *Keep Clear* space
in highway-yellow paint. Acceleration flings
us to the trees. Gravitation hurls us back again.

Freddie's Revenge, Body Rock, Stratosphere,
Miami Trip. A painted space,
a high-legged wooden chair, a woman
sitting there… Freddie's Revenge, Body
Rock, Stratosphere, Miami Trip.

Inside the crammed adrenaline, one Keep Clear
space in highway-yellow paint. Her lap's
a weight of change, her grip a bulb of hobbled
helium. Inside the crammed adrenaline,
one *Keep Clear* space in highway-yellow paint.

A painted space, a high-legged wooden
chair, a woman sitting there… Lighter
than air – rare – straining beyond Earth's
atmosphere. A painted space, a high-legged
wooden chair, a woman sitting there…

Her lap's a weight of change, her grip
a bulb of hobbled helium. This simple thing:
a boy – a coin – a balloon – and he lets go;
we watch it to a speck. Her lap's a weight
of change, her grip a bulb of hobbled helium.

Lighter than air – rare – straining beyond
Earth's atmosphere. And he lets go –
the simplest thing. It climbs without
adrenaline. Lighter than air – splits its skin –
moving beyond Earth's atmosphere.

Kevin Graham

Ivory Tower

Strange how a book always seemed to fall
on the same page, the rest turning to pulp.
Exams loomed like aggregated rainfall,
nerves fattening under pressure, the gulp

and slurp of waves on Malahide beach
a break from the same desk-jammed routine.
There, the seagulls floated just out of reach
the way all our future lives pine

to be heard over the racket of the heart.
The head at that age is an erratic skip
of mnemonic junk, learned-off facts
and quotations. Look how the years slip

like ferries on the brink of perfected sky.
I ask where all those fears ended up –
the sting that hid behind the question why;
the pause that filled an empty cup

at a party, girls spread-eagled over boys'
laps, French-kissing, the music going
like it would never stop. We were toys
in our parents' middle-aged lives, pride a song

that played in the stillness between breaths
so that studying meant proving the neighbours
wrong. Oh how we lost the little wreaths
of innocence that hung around our necks.

Stars hide your fires, went the phrase,
but ours were already hidden, the way
a good poem read out in English class
captured what we could never seem to say.

The Trigger

Tired from work, town humming with the panic
of evening shoppers, I pass through a clue
of perfume, skip fifteen years and am fifteen again,

agog that I could have walked through the village
along the coast with this creature at my side,
her Valentine's Day card fresh in my pocket,

hair bright, foreign as a dragonfly, skin on fire
from nervousness, those familiar places cast
in new light – clusters of weak saplings, sprawling

estates, the shop – a tribal tom-tom thrumming
in my chest loud as any brass band, the wishful sea
just out of reach, her hand a stroke away,

tongue now on mine, the world a spinning top
of Yeatsian visions and entangled truths, the sky
between breaths pink as the inside of a seashell,

the stars not yet out and still not old enough
to understand nostalgia or how a moment like this
can outlive the strange logic of its passing,

hang like a tattoo in the mind's eye and project
itself from the mirror into which you stare
with all the yearning of a boy in the body of a man.

Triptych in Memoriam

A Sighting

The club turns on its lights, its trendy clientele
and hot music. We stand at the bar
and order mojitos, crushed mint lingering on our
tongues. What's brought us out is not to dwell
on your not being here: the shadow
of lost company. So many nights we stayed
to kiss and dance and drink our lives away,
waking up sick and groggy and slow.

The DJ holds a headphone to his ear
as you – or someone who looks like you –
emerges from the fray: unshaven, you stare
out from the surrounding crowd, blue
eyes piercing the darkness and dry ice, creating
a kind of electricity out of nothing.

Martyn Crucefix

The Five Forward Prize First Collections

Mona Arshi: *Small Hands* (Liverpool University Press, Pavilion Poetry, 2015)
Sarah Howe: *Loop of Jade* (Chatto & Windus, 2015)
Andrew McMillan: *physical* (Cape Poetry, 2015)
Matthew Siegel: *Blood Work* (CB Editions, 2015)
Karen McCarthy Woolf: *An Aviary of Small Birds* (Carcanet, 2015).

Despite the ironic lack of capaciousness implied by its title, *Small Hands* is a brimming miscellany of poems. Many of them suggest interesting growing points for the future, but Sathnam Sanghera's claim that Arshi is 'Britain's most promising writer' and Moniza Alvi's talk of 'genius' is premature and liable to drag the reputation of blurb-writing even deeper into the mire. A trying-on of various recognisable styles or voices is expected of any first book, compiled as they usually are over years awaiting a publisher's call, but Arshi's arrival at a full collection has been swift. Publicity suggests she only turned from a profession in law to poetry around 2008. It's for this reason that her influences (Alvi, Petit and Khalvati most obviously, perhaps Emily Berry) are so clear.

Two early poems in the book allude to the idea of catastrophe. 'Practising Your Skills' faces an accusation about a 'tendency to catastrophise everything' and this also emerges in 'Bad Day in the Office' where the narrator is trying not to regard rainfall as 'catastrophic'. These instances may be 'character' points but such a ramping or ratchetting up of the ordinary is often evident elsewhere in the book and tends to caricature, a dramatic arc-lighting, unexpected (literally cata-stropic) links between disparate ideas or images and hence a love of listing: in other words, forms of surrealism. This is something Arshi has spoken about, regarding and admiring poetry as a discourse utterly counter to the kind of language-use she once employed in the law. So 'The Lion' is out of Angela Carter's *The Bloody Chamber* via Pascale Petit and evokes a strange relationship between a woman and an older man. It's a powerfully disturbing poem because the male figure is accorded such power, language, sensuality, wisdom and a sort of *droit de seigneur* over the female narrator who seems disinclined to question the set up. As with several of the quasi-pornographic pieces by Sam Rivière, the critical question here is where lies the irony? It is hard to tell, especially as this is the book's opener.

Arshi's somewhat whimsical surrealism is better seen in her portraits of female figures alone. 'Cousin Migrant' is a visitant 'from the skies' as well as a paradox ('her arms are thin as margins yet she can lift my children / with ease'). The Cousin's transgressive – or more accurately, indefinable qualities – are conveyed clearly and humourously; the narrator, in contrast, is nothing more than *a storm in a tea-cup*. The confines or otherwise of female lives are treated in more conventional poetic form in the object and memory piece, 'The Gold Bangles', evoked as a cultural inheritance of value though the narrator prefers to think of their owner's wrists *before* the gift, 'still unadorned and naked'. As here, there are several other poems that draw on Arshi's background, born to Punjabi Sikh parents in West London. 'Jesus Saves' is also a more conventional poem of childhood memory, on this occasion hearing a racist speaker in 1979, on Hounslow High Street, 'long after Enoch'. But elsewhere, Arshi prefers to construct enigmatic poems, hovering just beyond the edge of anything one might regard as a clear body of evidence. This is especially so in what seem to be 'relationship' poems like 'Entomological Specimens', 'Practising Your Skills' or 'Insomniac' which cryptically advises: 'Never marry an insomniac. You will have / to mind yourself'.

At the centre of the book are several poems about the tragic loss of Arshi's brother, Deepak, at the age of 41. These poems are moving and suggest contrasting aspects of her work such as deep levels of tact and restraint. Moving through the experiences of learning of his death and the family's adjustment to his loss in slant poems about a phone call, practical details of the mourning process, officialdom, the family garden, the urn, the loss still feels raw and unresolved and there will be more poems to come on this topic I'm sure.

The other prominent and enjoyable aspect of Arshi's work is its sensuality and awareness of the body; this is a collection full of hands, feet, mouths, lips, eyes, wrists, hair and, ubiquitously, skin. In 'Lost Poem' she talks of 'taking in language / through my skin' and there is a clear project developing here in that, at their best, these poems unfold through a language of the senses rather than the intellect. Elsewhere, Arshi writes of wanting to 'sequester' and 'foreignate' words, de-familiarising them, wresting them away from conventional denotation. I first heard her read aloud when she won the *Magma* Poetry Competition in 2011 with the ghazal-like poem, 'Hummingbird', here tucked away at the back of the book. I now read that poem against 'The Lion' and this is the one I prefer for its originality. The narrative voice (undefined) addresses the 'you' which is mostly the hummingbird itself, though as with 'The Lion' the creature is also interchangeably / metaphorically human. The tender, persuasive imperatives almost immediately carry an erotic charge, though where the 'fingers' probe and slip is mostly into 'spaces', lacunae. But the hummingbird figure has none of the over-bearing masculinity of the lion; we are told it is capable of 'curing', dissolving, even pronouncing the speaker. But the speaker here is not as passive and compliant as in the earlier poem. Though she will allow him/her to open the 'bone-zip of my spine', the insistence of her voice gives her an active role in the relationship. The hummingbird is invited to 'anoint' the speaker, a significant contrast to the shallowness of the lion's crude 'undressing'.

George Szirtes' rather more restrained comments suggest that he reads in Arshi's work an 'erotics of the spirit'. Without doubt, 'The Hummingbird' is a sexy, enigmatic, yet precisely expressed poem that is going to repay our re-reading of it. And if that is not the case with many other poems in *Small Hands* we should not be surprised. Arshi combines a liking for obliqueness, sometimes even coolness, with a desire to push what language can do and a willingness to experiment with form. Her cultural background is relatively unexplored here, yet promises much if that is the way she wishes to go. Not a winner of the 2015 Forward First Book award for me, but an intriguing writer, potentially a unique voice if she can achieve the right distance between herself and her powerful formative influences.

Sarah Howe's first full collection is packed with journeys, stories, bits of language, calligraphy, mothers and daughters – but mostly it should be admired for its readiness to experiment. The concluding poem, 'Yangtze', might be read as an evocation of the Daoist belief in the primacy of fluidity and the watercourse way. A moon glimmers uncertainly on water's surfaces, a river flows, a diving bird vanishes into it, fishermen's nets catch on something submerged, a bridge remains only 'half-built', a travelling boat merely 'points' to its destination. What remains hidden and inarticulate predominates; as the *Daodejing* argues, our life's journey often runs against the current because we mostly lack the proper perspective to see the world is really one, not the parts we think we know. Those eighty one wonderful ancient Chinese poems also argue that our way forward is really backwards, to *recover* an understanding of what has always been: that sense of unity of being which underlies all phenomena. Their wisdom is a sort of nostalgia and this is what drives much of Howe's work.

Two nostalgic tributaries flow into *Loop of Jade* – one philosophical, the other autobiographical. As in Daoist thought, words are not to be relied on and this is why Howe's epigraph is by Borges, out of Foucault. It is a mock absurd taxonomy of the animal kingdom, sub-divided into a) belonging to the emperor, b) embalmed, c) tame, and so on to n) that from a long way off look like flies. The butt of the joke is language's categories, organised perhaps in such quasi-random ways. Several poems play with the pleasant thought that Chinese calligraphy can bring us closer to the truth. A scholar sits in his study and 'lends his brush the ideal pressure – / leaves his mind there, on the paper'. Jesuit missionaries arriving at Canton likewise thought they'd discovered 'Adam's perfect tongue', the language of Eden, an 'anchoring of sign to thing'. The poems address the risk that we 'might forget // words' tenuous moorings' but as we are all signed-up postmodernists nowadays the joke ends at the scholar-poet's expense in the poem *'(k) Drawn with a very fine camelhair brush'* when his poorly tethered boat drifts away and leaves him helplessly marooned upstream.

Yet Howe is poet enough ('poet-scholar' is more of a disjunction than a working synthesis) to allow a woman in a Bonnard painting to long for 'someone who will teach her the names of trees' ('Woman in the Garden') and the technique of the banderole – those speech scrolls often included in paintings – makes an unusual subject for a poem because it is a way to 'make / mute canvas speak' ('Banderole'). Perhaps it even bears some resemblance to Chinese calligraphy. Certainly, we need names as a form of geography, 'for knowing where we are and names / of fixed and distant things' ('Islands'). Accordingly, Howe scatters brief lyric poems, mostly descriptive, through the book and these seem also to aspire towards the state of calligraphy – one way at least of negotiating with the recalcitrance, the difficulty of mooring words; but these are not among the most successful poems in the book.

Instead, Howe's experimentalism is more iconoclastic as shown in *'(m) Having just broken the water pitcher'*. This poem draws on a story from Wumen Huikai's *The Gateless Gate* in which the sage Baizhang asks his pupil 'If you cannot call it a water pitcher, what do you call it?' The correct reply, we are told, is to kick the pitcher over and leave! There are some fascinating insights buried in this book about the rebelliousness of Chinese bloggers reinventing forms of language to avoid censorship and there's no doubt they can be seen as partaking in the ancient traditions of their country. To paraphrase the opening chapter of the *Daodejing*: the words you are permitted to use are not the words that will remain. The kicked-over pitcher – to shift the metaphor as the *Daodejing* does – breaks the paradigm, returns us to the uncarved block of wood, the original state, before words, government, censorship.

This original state is characterised in Laozi's Dao poems as the 'mother of all' and the second nostalgic tributary flowing powerfully into Howe's book is an autobiographical exploration of her Chinese mother's life and culture. This is the more immediately accessible and marketable thread of the book that the Chatto blurb draws attention to and these poems are very vivid and moving. Most of them build in a documentary style, full of specific, often period, details to demonstrate yet another way of negotiating between words and things. 'Crossing from Guangdong' (a poem that might be usefully read beside Elizabeth Bishop's 'Arrival at Santos') has the narrator arriving on a paradoxically 'strange pilgrimage to home', trying to imagine her mother's earlier life:

> Something sets us looking for a place.
> Old stories tell that if we could only
> get there, all distances would be erased

This search is as much philosophical/spiritual as autobiographical: 'Soon we will reach / the fragrant city', though arriving at the putative destination, there is still so much 'you can no longer see'. The title sequence of the book itself is in this mode, becoming even more documentary in its largely prose passages, interspersed with lyrical folk tale material and ventriloquistic evocations of the mother's speaking voice. It ends with a more conventional poem on the jade pendant itself, given by the mother, blessed by a grandmother. It is worn to protect: 'if baby // falls, the loop of stone – a sacrifice – / will shatter / in her place'. Curiously, the final line suggests some sort of fall has already taken place though the jade remains intact and I guess this is the fall from cultural roots torn up in Howe's childhood move to the West: 'And if I break it now – will I be saved?'

This is a fecund book, full of poetic ideas and a variety of forms. But it's not exactly easy reading. Howe isn't always inclined to swing her poems far across the chasm between writer and reader. But their richness derives from the twin sources of Howe's thinking: on one side erudite and philosophical, on the other intimate and autobiographical and the use she makes of the myths, thinkers, stories and landscapes of her Chinese background means this is a book unlike any other.

A man's torso, from just below the shoulder to half-way down the rounded buttocks, tastefully lit from the back to catch the curves, his left hand visible clutching (quite hard) his own right flank. It's sexy and lonely and longing and anonymous. It's a bit *Fifty Shades* but Cape Poetry's cover image does say something about Andrew McMillan's first full collection, though it's too confining. It's the sort of sharply targeted thing marketing people come up with and the author (who is achieving cleanly-shaped, clear, bold things in terms of subject-matter and form) may squirm at.

But the image is flauntingly male (and happily the skin blemishes have not been air-brushed) and what it is to be a man is certainly one of McMillan's concerns. In 'strongman' a nephew wants to be bench-pressed by the male narrator and (even from the young child) this is a clear challenge as 'his mother's lover' often does it, the boy has declared the narrator's boyfriend 'illegal' and he brings with him the freight of traditional masculine values: 'his dad's voice and jaw'. The narrator obliges 'because / what is masculinity if not taking the weight // of a boy and straining it from oneself?' It's not just the bench-press requiring careful balance here in the close masculine contact, the show of strength, the carefully maintained distance in the preposition 'from'. The inculcation of traditional male values starts early as in 'The Schoolboys' who clamber onto a bus, all bulge and muscle and 'sprints of growth', wrestling 'to impress the girls'. The poem 'things men take' is one of McMillan's lists, articulating a more adult version of this: they take 'the room above the ceiling / the better pay the jobs / your space at the bar'. But it's with a poem like 'the men are weeping in the gym' that we begin to see this poet's determination to challenge the status quo in its brief fantasy of male affectiveness: 'their hearts have grown too big / for their chests their chests have grown too big / for their shirts... they are crying in the toilet'. There is real humour here as the gym is turned from a place of physical exercise to a place where emotions are released and flexed, a re-definition of those traditional ideas of 'strength': 'they don't hear / the thousands of tiny fracturings / needed to build something stronger'.

But masculinity as in what it is to be a gay man in love is even more central to *physical*. A definition of love emerges at the end of one poem which begins with awkward fears of (literally) bumping into men in a urinal, causing spillage, splash, a turning, the revelation: 'neither of us will look / or he'll look at me avoiding looking / feigning interest in the hard cream tiles'. This is funny again though halfway through the bluntly titled 'urination', McMillan considers the privacy and intimacy of 'the toilet', the poem lifting into praise of waking to hear (and smell) a lover pissing 'the morning's pale yellow loss' into the toilet 'and take the whole of him in your hand / and feel the water moving through him'. Such intimacy of contact is one of the provisional definitions of love: 'the prone flesh / what we expel from the body and what we let inside'. Poems that explore the physicality of the male body make this book remarkable, even given McMillan's acknowledged debt to Thom Gunn. Much after the pattern of 'urination', 'yoga' begins with the physical stretching and breathing of the class, but shades seamlessly into a love-making which echoes the breath, control, weightlessness and absence of 'judgement' in the discipline of yoga. 'Saturday night' takes lines from Gunn's poem of that name, this time to explore a more roaming, disjointed experience of love and sexuality. The rule of 'Boss Cupid' is no more reliable than in the straight world, of course, and McMillan gives us other images of sleeping with 'Thom night after night / open at the spine', rather than any flesh and blood lover. And 'screen' imagines how even a gay porn star, so perfect and capable on screen, in real life 'without direction' struggles to express himself, 'stopping mid kiss pulling back mumbling'.

As my quotes suggest, McMillan abandons most punctuation in these poems, using only line and stanza breaks and long spaces to create pauses and some sense of syntactical form. This works well – it doesn't for me interrupt or confuse at all – and contributes to the often passionate flow of the poems. It's hard to convey this in short quotes but 'choke', running for just twenty two lines, takes us rapidly through a relationship break-up, weeping, talking, loving and next day reflections, managing to evoke the agitation, fluidity of feelings, and final resolve 'to tough it out' and the lack of pointing is part of this success. Elsewhere, the flow and even blurring achieved syntactically is just right for the loss of self-consciousness associated with sexual pleasure.

What is interesting is that beside the passionate and 'carnal' (Michael Symmons Robert's word) nature of much of this book and alongside Thom Gunn as mentor and role model, McMillan also refers to C.S. Lewis' *Mere Christianity*. The opening poem of the book portrays gay sexuality with Jacob wrestling the angel and I've mentioned the paralleling in 'yoga' and those beefy men crying in the gym are said to have 'God' entering them as they weep. Furthermore, 'revelations' argues that each subsequent love is only a searching for the first, 'in the manner of the humble saints who make / the worship of a nameless god relatable'. Each lover is renamed, 'Saint Gavin Saint Ged Saint Unknown / of Manchester Bedsit'. Humour is used here but it hardly disguises the poet's interest in the more spiritual implications of the physicality his poems work so hard to evoke. This religious sensibility emerges in the brief foray, moving from Eros towards Thanatos, in poems in the third part of the book. The deaths of a grandfather and a young girl strike a very different note and suggest that McMillan may have found in Gunn not merely ways to explore his own sexuality in verse but also (from early Gunn) that existential sense, so wonderfully expressed in 'On the Move' (1957), that movement (whether on a motor bike or in bed) is at least one way towards self-definition: 'astride the created will / They burst away... Reaching no absolute in which to rest, / One is always nearer by not keeping still'.

There is something of this in the final poem of *physical*. Ironically titled 'finally', it evokes a new morning in 'the xylophone / of sunthroughblinds', but the lover is gone, not to return and the poet is like the birds who, though it hasn't rained, pretend that it has, so 'they can sing'. Earlier, the longer sequence 'protest of the physical' noted 'there is beauty in the ordinary' but this is a pallid observation in contrast to this poet's determination towards self-definition through loving, through singing when the loving is over.

In a collection full of humour and sadness alongside the plain-spoken eroticism, I really like what McMillan is doing with the fluidity of his form. I don't think the longer sequence 'protest of the physical' is as good as the other sections of the book (I believe it preceded them in terms of date written) but here is a really talented and bold writer and I can see further areas of exploration opening up and it will be exciting to follow him there.

Matthew Siegel's book is a really good first collection because of its remarkable consistency of tone and manner and it possesses what I, perhaps narrow-mindedly think of, as that American quality of confident fluency, indeed fluidity, which seems capable of encompassing so much experience without straining at the seams. In their very different ways, I find this in the work of poets like Billy Collins, Louise Glück, Jorie Graham, Robert Hass and Larry Levis. I'd trace it back to the big enfolding arms and lines of Whitman who, along with Rilke, are Siegel's two declared influences. But this 'all I survey' quality of the book is rather undermined by the publicity surrounding it which narrowly focuses on the fact that Siegel was diagnosed at the age of sixteen with Crohn's disease and that his debut collection is all about this. Mark Doty considers the book 'a genuine contribution to the literature of illness'.

It may well be – but like Robert Lowell, Thom Gunn and more recently Dan O'Brien, *Blood Work*'s focus on a very specific milieu or set of experiences does not prevent the alchemical transformation into an art with which those not brought up in the upper reaches of New England society, in the West Coast gay scene, embroiled in modern war zones can identify. In old money terms, they find the universal in the particular and Siegel does this in poems that move beyond a young American with Crohn's disease to explore family relations, love relationships, questions of self-definition and the tensions between speech and silence.

The opening poem is important in carving out a certain distance, an ironic space, between the Crohn's sufferer and the poetic voice (there are a few ekphrastic poems scattered through the book which do the same job). It is one of the few poems narrated in the third person and we are urged to 'look' at a hospital attendee, back in what seems familiar territory (the chronic aspect of Crohn's), the floral prints on the walls, the hospital gown 'like an old costume / pulled out of a locked trunk in the attic / of bad dreams'. He feels sexless or desexualised, but is writing a poem 'in lowercase', particularly the first person pronoun. The writing of the poem becomes the subject of the poem but this self-reflectiveness is not rebarbative in the way it often can be (self-regarding, aggrandising, clever-clever) but more modestly self-mocking, an awkward self-consciousness. The patient/poet would rather be drawing a comic book, with himself as a 'small mammal'. He sees himself as a fox and in the poem's final line he changes the title of the poem he is writing which is the title at the head of the first page we have just read: 'fox goes to the fox hospital'.

The space created by this poem around the very specific medical context gives the remaining book permission to range widely and introduces the idea of 'containment'. What can or cannot contain the individual is a recurring idea (picked up by Doty in the cover blurb). The title poem has the narrator's blood being taken from a vein (already a familiar experience to this young man – the context seems to be earlier in the poet's life). The nurse allows him to hold the warm filled tubes of his own blood: 'I nod, think about condoms, tissues / all the things that contain us but cannot'. Containment here means summation perhaps, but with overtones of imprisonment in the sense that a medical condition (a disability? a gender? a skin colour?) may determine much about the individual, yet ought not be allowed to fully define the person. This too is Siegel's subject in the book; the spillage, or extension, we can achieve or are permitted beyond what might define us.

So 'Sometimes I don't know if I'm having a feeling' may or may not be closely related to the poet's own medical condition but it is a familiar experience for most of us. The uncertainty of thoughts and feelings, the sensation of having missed 'the entire party', of being known only as 'a strange / version of the person you thought you knew', the old question, 'Who am I?' It's a sign of the ironic distance maintained by these poems (not at all the same as cool inconsequentiality) that Siegel can answer that question with humour: 'A question / for the Lord only to decide as She looks over / my resumé'. Elsewhere, such questions are more difficult to answer. 'Love Parade' stresses the distance the narrator feels from others ('I fear my body incapable of loving') or he plays with the idea that the opportunity of a poem is little more than a late-night phone-in for the lost and lonely. The desire for contact with others (that wish for spillage and extension) can grow to 'the size of a building', taking Siegel down avenues of surrealistic imagery, creating a city-scape from the thoughts of a lover's body.

These 'others' do feature significantly in this book. We meet the heater repair woman, a Vietnamese masseuse, Nancy the dentist, a supermarket flower seller, stall-holders at a Farmer's Market, a multitude of doctors and nurses, various romantic entanglements. Though all these dip and dance about the central consciousness, they are given individuality (more Whitman here, I think). Thirteen year old Bryan is a sleepy student and the narrator is the teacher who watches him doze at his desk, bored by a literature class. The poem is a lovely act of empathy with the boy, his awkwardness and uncertainties, concluding with the self-discovery that the boy may well become the watching adult who 'instead of chastising him / wants to touch his hair'.

But the book is also concerned with family, in particular a mother-figure who, like Bryan, is observed while sleeping and Siegel asks 'What world / contains you'. In this poem, she dozes, exhaling 'in little puffs' and perhaps it is her son's inability to quite define her that means he can 'only watch for so long'. She is a mystery, though in poem after poem she is shown crying, smoking dope to forget, mourning an ex-fiancé, the son helplessly left to 'wonder if I could reassemble my mother'. In 'Matthew you're leaving again so soon' we hear her reported voice fussing and trying to bestow love and affection through gifts of pens, an umbrella, socks, as he prepares to leave, in an effort to say what seems impossible to be said explicitly. We see her (smoking another joint) listening to the music of Enya ('it's in Gaelic'), tearful again, yet smiling 'as if hurt is the balm'. For all the lack of specific detail about her life and loves, this mother-figure is a powerful creation we may hear more of in Siegel's later work.

So the book does not duck difficult experiences, nor distance them defensively. Siegel's watchwords are openness and a winning tenderness. Despite the questions of illness, he can apply such qualities to himself too and in 'Overlooking the City' there is a brief respite which amounts to something like redemption: 'No, I am not hurting in this moment'. As the sun sets over the city, 'red does not remind me of blood' and the imagined blessing of the sun's rays reach 'even me, surrounded here and alone'.

Even in a poem that gets pretty explicit about his medical condition, some reconciliation seems possible. 'Rain' opens:

> I thought I knew desperation until I found myself
> tightening my asshole like a bolt,
> gripping the banister and crossing both legs,
> knees shaking.
> I tried to read a poem on the toilet...

But still the narrator can elude such a total, imprisoning self-definition to find some pleasure in the view from a window to 'see grass // glowing green in rain and streetlight – / so many bright beads of water'.

This is a book I really admire for its capacity to encompass such variety without bursting into fragmentary utterances. It doesn't do anything startling formally or linguistically, but its achievement is more emotional and empathetic, Siegel's voice engages the reader at all times in just the way he seems to engage and commit to the many people who inhabit these poems with him.

Carcanet's colourful cover image of fluttering songbirds belies the terrific freight of grief that Karen McCarthy Woolf's book carries. The poems are presented as highly autobiographical and there are actually three deaths involved: that of a friend from cancer, a mother-in-law, and the central focus is the stillbirth of the author's son in August 2009. The very personal nature of the materials makes critical discussion difficult but, in reading the poems, I found myself thinking of T S Eliot's observations about what he regarded as the failure of *Hamlet*. This is the 1919 essay in which Eliot proposes his idea of the objective correlative, 'a set of objects, a situation, a chain of events which shall be the formula of [a] particular emotion'. The emotion is re-evoked in the reader when the objective correlative is supplied by the writer. But Eliot argues Shakespeare could never quite unearth or disentangle the true emotions which he hoped would empower the play's chain of events of a father's untimely death and a mother's remarriage.

McCarthy Woolf's book suggests something quite the opposite in that the specific emotions and key events of the child's death always form the underlying premise on which every single one of these poems runs. This is both a strength and a weakness. The problem can be seen in 'The Sooty Shearwaters' which plainly describes the birds heading out to sea to feed. Their return at night time is aided by the switching off of TVs and streetlamps so the birds can 'navigate by starlight / to find their young'. The birds' cry is unique we are told; DJs come to sample it. But what the poem gives us is a chain of events, an objective correlative, which fails to evoke a strong response unless and until the reader brings to the poem the prior knowledge of the stillborn child's loss. Only when apprised of that does the shearwaters' determined, instinctive return to their young (and the island population's touching assistance to that end) really gain force.

Also, as an exploration of the experience of grief, the book faces inevitable limitations because of the nature of the loss. There are several poems set in the acute moments surrounding the stillbirth and immediately afterwards but the majority are set sometime later (the book was six years in the making). Poems are arranged in a broadly chronological fashion and in an interesting reflection of the way a reader must keep in mind the premise of the original loss, many of the poems record the mother's inability to move on from that same loss so that she, and the world around her, is repeatedly haunted by it. There are powerful moments here to be sure but no broadening religious dimension (Tennyson's *In Memoriam*), no political thread (Tony Harrison's *The School of Eloquence*), nor can there be any development (other than speculatively) about the nature of the lost one as in Hardy's 1912 poems, Douglas Dunn's *Elegies*, Anne Carson's *Nox*, or Rilke's *Requiem for a*

Friend. The utterly tragic nature of the child's loss in stillbirth imposes its own limits on the artistic response.

Nevertheless, *An Aviary of Small Birds* is admirably experimental in formal terms, some successful, others reading (surprisingly) like exercises carried out. For example, 'The Museum of Best Laid Plans' is a prose listing of the items on a bedside shelving unit, ending with a lock of infant hair. In contrast, 'Morbleu' takes us into the panic-stricken, semi-chaos of the delivery room, which is frighteningly conveyed through typographical layout and spacing: '– we haven't got – / a heart beat'. These are examples of the poems that stand up well independently, communicating fully to any reader whether in the context of this intensely-focused collection or not. Some of the best and most moving of other pieces take a markedly tangential approach to the tragic circumstances (perhaps the only way to approach such a grief). So 'The Paperwork' focuses on filling in a post-mortem form and makes powerful use of the tone and language of formality and administration so that one of the last options to be considered acquires, by contrast, even greater emotional weight: 'Eyes not to be touched. / The doctor bites her lip, writes it in the box'. 'The Registrar's Office' also manages to contain and convey its grief through indirectness as the bereaved mother, in a lightly punctuated flow and flurry of words, unburdens herself to the Registrar, but ends being more concerned about the windowless room in which the woman works. This illogical transference of the mother's grief to a separate object is clear and credible and powerfully communicated to the reader.

What the book does not offer in a sustained fashion is a more forensic analysis of grief, its impact and evolution; it says mainly that grief does not go away. 'Where Steel Clatters' is a strong poem describing a threatening-seeming landscape of whining saws, bullet holes, 'a burnt-out Renault' – but the bereaved mother is únmoved by it, having learned that 'the worst things happen in brash, / fluorescent rooms where steel clatters / and silence is the total absence of movement'. 'Starlight' is a curbed, curtailed, halting poem – as if it were weighed down by grief – expressing more directly the desire to be 'away / from the gurney // and the empty metal cot'. It is perhaps through experiences with the natural world that some sort of consolation begins to be felt. 'The Calf' is set off the Canary Islands and makes untypical but important use of the islanders' mythic belief that 'the animal you need // always comes to you'. What the bereaved mother wants is to swim with a pilot whale calf, though this is 'against the law'. There is a sighting from a boat: 'then he's gone // down into the dark. / Something is better than nothing'. In fact, the poem, which has surely ended here, goes on for another four lines (over a page break) and there are a few other moments where a final edit might have been considered.

McCarthy Woolf has great empathy with the many animals in her poems and not only concerning the bird motif that runs through the collection. A dead hawk lying in a stream provides some 'comfort' in a godless and faithless age; the 'return to water, to the stream, to the earth' suggests some sort of cycle of life motif. And this is one of the most moving aspects of these poems of contemporary grief – the signal lack of outlets or rituals that might serve as ways of dealing with the loss. Latterly, rivers are imagined as speaking of the need to 'endure' and the title poem itself redeploys the image of the lost child as a small bird in an aviary. The instinct of the natural creature, its need to be let go, is what teaches right action to the atomised, isolated, faithless individual of the mother in this book: though there is precious little evidence of moving-on to be found in the collection, there is a realisation that it will be achieved only when the mother learns 'to leave the door ajar'.

Critical comment feels inappropriate at times with this book but it is presented to the reader as a poetry collection, not a memoir. There is, throughout, a reaching for poetic variety not wholly matched by a variety of perspectives on the fundamental grief portrayed. There are several very powerful poems which I admire as technical achievements (given the powerful emotions from which they are derived, I don't mean that as faint praise). But there are also a few make-weight pieces. McCarthy Woolf, whose book runs to only sixty three pages, might, even so, have learned from the ultra-brevity and resultingly intense focus and consistency of a book like Colette Bryce's *The Whole and Rain-domed Universe* (Picador), which weighed in last year at just forty nine pages.

W S Milne

New Generation Poets

Abegail Morley: *The Memory of Water* (Indigo Pamphlets, 2015)
Kate Miller: *The Observances* (Oxford*Poets*, Carcanet, 2015)
Richie McCaffery: *Spinning Plates* (Happenstance, 2012)
Anna Lewis: *Other Harbours* (Parthian Poetry, 2012)
Anna Lewis: *The Blue Cell* (Rack Press, 2015)
Sean Borodale: *Human Work* (Cape Poetry, 2015)
Helen Mort: *Division Street* (Chatto Poetry, 2013)
Rebecca Goss: *Her Birth* (Northern House, Carcanet, 2013)
Wendy Pratt: *Lapstrake* (Flarestack Poets, 2015)
Sarah Sibley: *The Withering Room* (Green Bottle Press, 2015)
Isabel Galleymore: *Dazzle Ship* (Worple Press, 2014)

There appear to be no new schools of poetry. The age of manifestoes (perhaps thankfully) is over. Poets once liked to form groups, circles, movements, schools. Think of the Symbolists, the Vorticists, the Georgians, the Imagists, the Mavericks, the Concrete Poets, and so on. Young contemporary poets don't seem to go in for this form of congregating. When they gather it is not to form *isms* but to discuss the value of their poetry in workshops and discussion groups. This can be of great technical value, and further the intricacies of their craft. The process or procedure ensures a healthy diversity in contemporary verse, a plethora of styles and voices. One doesn't have to march in line with everybody else. The downside, possibly, is that each poet has to scramble to find or establish their own voice – they are not following a leading idea or concept. And finding your own poetic voice within 'the field of rules' (Jorie Graham's phrase) is the hardest task of all. You have to absorb, and then cast off, the centuries of voices which have preceded you. This is the sure sign of a mature poet, a distinct, irrefutable voice, a personality like no other. The apprenticeship is served, you can strike out on your own – it's more than just 'skating on the surface', it is plumbing the depths (this is the way Abegail Morley sees it in her poem 'What the moat knows'), making the living word dance and sing. So poems are not mere 'skeletons' to be disturbed and exhumed (think perhaps of the Modernists' over-reliance on literary quotations, all those borrowed voices in Eliot and MacDiarmid) but a living history to be explored. Without a 'school' behind you, this can be a scary undertaking. And therein lies the bravery, the courage, of contemporary young poets. They have to pit their vision against so many others in a climate not always conducive to poetry. It is a lone discipline conducted in an often unfriendly environment. The miracle is that poetry survives at all, but survive it does in such publications as are here under review.

The Memory of Water is Abegail Morley's fourth collection, and the poems are complemented with fine photographs by Karen Dennison. William Bedford has written that 'these poems bring vivid life to actual voices of the past and counterpoints them with invented characters', the sequence chiefly concerned with the empirical effect whereby 'When you add a substance to water and then dilute the water to the point where there are no more molecules of the added substance left in the water, you can still measure effects of the water as if the originally diluted substance were still present' – the poet calls this effect 'the water's mechanics'. The result is ghostly, spectral, providing Morley with interesting analogies throughout the pamphlet: 'the world has touched us, scars//not quite healed', she writes, establishing unlikely connections between phenomena in 'the slow press of time', 'somehow bound together like a bridge//spanning a harbour', breaking down (as Yeats so often did) geophysical and psychical distances. Again, like Yeats in his tower, Morley captures the spooky memories haunting the castle she inhabits, presences such as recusants hiding in priest-holes where she 'can smell the scent of her ancestors' like a spoor. Her intimations are built on tradition and convention ('how foundations sought/a stronghold in the earth' she writes). Poetic structure therefore holds Heraclitean flux in place as 'Sandstone learns the meaning of water,/how it can slow down, hold onto itself', the poet's solitary vigil noting how 'time/ nudges itself forward like/a lost thought recovered'. Poetry therefore helps to overcome the terrible vortex of time and death, opposing decay by creating 'a small circle of light' within the surrounding darkness and emptiness – the poet launching out on the great sea of being like 'a deep sea fishing boat slipping harbour'. It is a perilous journey, a dangerous undertaking, for nothing is certain, nothing secure. The poet's 'still small voice' (see the poem of that title, borrowed from *Kings*) stems the world's corruption. The coarse materials of the world, including language itself, have to be transformed into art – the art of poetry as embodied here. The varying states of water, its metamorphoses (vapour, liquid, gas, drizzle, fog, ice, rain, streams, clouds, a moat) represent the shiftings of the world, the kinesis against which the stasis of poetry is set. The poet has to weed out 'all fake, hoodwink, humbug' ('Do not trust water,//it's a performer, cousin of winter,/fault lines, dying stars') by realizing the 'utter uncertainty /in language' and redeeming that uncertainty through 'the drab burden of words'. Nature has to be tamed by art. *The Memory of Water* is a marvellous pamphlet of poems, and I highly recommend it.

The title of Kate Miller's book, *The Observances* (an echo, perhaps, of Marianne Moore's *Observations*?) leads us into poems of close, amplified concentration (Sarah Dugdale has called her focus 'the art of seeing', and Richard Price 'rituals of seeing'). The poet, like Rilke, is 'charged with witnessing', with breaking 'through the wall of mourning'. Like Morley, Miller is fully aware of convention ('I brace to take the weight of tradition' she states) but I'm not sure she is as successful as Morley in this regard. A poem often requires more than just close observation (Rilke himself, in 'Sonnets to Orpheus', said 'There is a limit to what can be achieved by gazing...') But I think nevertheless Miller has learned from the likes of Marianne Moore and Elizabeth Bishop that close witnessing can engage the reader for a while: 'Herons tilt in blue-grey river light/stab a crumpled eel', 'Steam for a bonfire. Slight rain advances/over glass, greasing the silence'. Each day, each moment, is a vigil for the poet, praising mundane objects such as 'nails, rope, bucket, knife', searching as the Objectivists did for the quiddity of the earth ('even this poor ground is inexhaustible' she says), discovering all that is best in the physical universe. Interested in 'every cast of light', Miller at the same time realizes the necessity for craft to ensure emotion doesn't overspill content. My favourite poem here is a lovely vignette of Rome called 'Against the Light'.

Richie McCaffery is a poet to look out for. *Spinning Plates* is an impressive inaugural pamphlet. The verse possesses an unadorned, undeceived style, a tough Scottish grit which has nothing captious or artificial about it, the makar's concentration on words as close and focused as that on the world surrounding him. It seems to me that McCaffery is a very fine poet in the gruff manner of Robin Robertson, and I can safely claim there is not a dud poem to be found in this pamphlet, the craft pared to the bone – bare, exact, austere (e.g. 'Dead flies gather on the windowsill like raisins'). There is a crisp, ardent concision, a new type of imagism at work here (possibly borrowed from his studies in Scottish literature) which is fresh and invigorating, containing raw social bite, which reminded me of early Geoffrey Hill or the *Odes* of Basil Bunting. McCaffery catches 'the shadow of the branch' exactly as William Faulkner recommended, everything being drawn obliquely with fine artistic tact, as in 'The truth so far':

In the chalky trough under the blackboard,
lessons dusted and already forgotten.

The teacher is squawking away once more,
scratching into the *tabula rasa*

the truths so far about God and arithmetic
with the expungible white of fossil shells.

The title of the sequence may seem odd, but is explained. His mother 'said being pregnant/was like spinning a bone-china plate/on the thinnest stick inside you – //breakages were bound to occur', a rather strange 'take'you might say on a miscarriage! The exact use of unusual words (netsukes, paregoric, cilices, canola) reminded me of the strategies of David Jones and Wallace Stevens, demonstrating that McCaffery understands the first duty of the poet to be a lover of words, to understand their 'chemistry'. He always seems to be able to find the exact object for the right emotion: house, whistle, chalk, cigarettes, postcards, teeth, rust, toys, a tent, a dead mouse, islands, spoons, plates, a handbag, a butterfly, a nose-ring – they are all 'objective correlatives' for deep emotion, close observation and tense thought (e.g. death is 'the keyless oubliette', a phrase worthy of Pascal himself).

Anna Lewis too is a fine phrasemaker, evident in her booklet, *The Blue Cell*, a chronicle of early Welsh saints and their purported miracles: 'the world webbed in ice' is particularly fine, as is the phrase 'a salmon longer than my arm'. However, her greater achievement is in her longer sequence, *Other Harbours*, where, like Morley and Miller, she opposes decay and decomposition 'with a new flame' of inspiration. Patrick McGuinness has written of 'the quiet, disconcerting precision' of her poems which explore and map 'new and tender contours' of the mind, and I think this is a fine comment. Lewis is another writer fully aware of the importance of tradition ('to understand what made the Minotaur steam in his cave' she writes) and I am glad to see she is not afraid of employing the long line (something learned perhaps from the practices of Jorie Graham?) as the majority of poets are. She is frighteningly aware of the solitariness of the profession ('I am alone in my corner' she says) and is much concerned with the diasporas of modern life, writing poems about England, Ireland, Wales, Anatolia, Tibet, Germany, Japan, China, a more cosmopolitan outlook perhaps than older generations possessed, always crossing boundaries, travelling in the globalised world, 'feet leaping the threshold without hesitation'. She views these journeys in a positive, life-enhancing way, not concentrating on the fractured nature of modern life but embracing it in all its diversity. She believes in 'the tinder and the ready fuse' of inspiration (possibly thinking of Dylan Thomas' 'The force that through the green fuse drives the flower'?), 'the lantern's ever-closer flame', of poems pitched against corruption and decay, searching for the spring, the well, of creativity: 'a long torso of water far underground,/sightless, burrowing up to the light'.

She presents us with a sequence of poems on famous Welsh heroes' wives from the *Mabinogion*, owing much to Carol Ann Duffy's *The World's Wife*, with a similarly charged eroticism, concentrating on the overlooked female voices in the Welsh epic. Her powers of observation are as acute as those poets mentioned above: here she is on lizards, for example: 'They barely breathe; a pulse flits/at the crux of their throats...' Anna Lewis is very aware that out of tradition the poet needs to make a new start, to avoid stagnation: 'Floors swept, litter plucked', she says, it is time to rid the town of 'old men'.

Human Work rides on the back of the current mania for kitchen culture, but in an interesting way. The book comprises a series of disturbing recipes portrayed like the Dutch realist school of painting, blood dripping from meat, apples gleaming in the sun, vegetables split open on oak tables. There is a debt here again I feel to the physicality of Robin Robertson's poetry (the opening poem owes far too much to Robertson, and he acknowledges the Scottish poet's help in the end-notes to the book). Although Borodale's first book was highly praised by Carol Ann Duffy, Simon Armitage, Alice Oswald, and Gillian Clarke, I am not entirely sure of the consistency of this collection. The problem I feel lies in the voyeuristic stress on butchery and brutality which dominates the volume. The genesis seems to lie in J M Synge's belief that 'before verse can be human again it must learn to be brutal' or Rilke's statement that 'killing is one of the forms of our homeless grief', but I'm not entirely convinced. Ted Hughes and Sylvia Plath surely covered this territory in more than enough depth. The poet states that he is 'riddling this tumbling dark with human work' but much of the work seems to be horribly psychopathic. Original sin ('the ancient edge of a deathbed') is never far from Borodale's imagination, his obsession with the 'disconnect' between ourselves and the world, our exile from Eden, evident from the first poem onwards. It is 'the sharpened stone of consciousness', our murderous, killing appetites, which grasp the poet's interest, Cain always ready to murder, the poet 'a ranger of the dispossessed'. History for Borodale is 'The knock of the axe, of the echo; the hum of flies'; 'Hunger is spooky' because it is never satisfied, never fulfilled (one thinks of James Joyce's view that the world is all hunter and hunted). Cooking is likened 'to the sweat after a murder'; a bream 'is the comb of the spine,/and there are bones like bodkins... We leave just salvage, the boat's ribs'. He is a primitivist, fascinated, like Ted Hughes, with the kipper's 'hook, hole, flesh, eye, fins, translucent lips' carved up in 'this cave of the kitchen'. But not all is bloody, for like Kate Miler he is searching (admittedly in a more savage way) for the haecceity of life in 'All hollow, holy objects' (the echo here, of course, is to the word 'hallowed'). As to my earlier mention of psychopathy,

I refer readers to the lines 'Beans, I kept/– like a killer keeps a corpse –/in the freezer for months' (a hint here surely of Hannibal Lecter's liking for eating fava beans and chianti with his victims?) and to the phrase, 'the trash of the boil' which is redolent of Beckett's story 'Dante and the Lobster'. Borodale is not unaware of tradition, however, referring to it as 'the long road with the dusty dead', 'a slow whirlpool of generations', 'damaged words'. 'I sensed/a clear, small miracle was being carried/under the depth of language' he writes, and it is this glimpse of salvation that redeems the almost interminable Hughesian slaughter, the dark butchery of the soul and 'the hurtling house' of the body. Poetry is seen as pitched against 'the looseness of a life', imagination's 'phantasmal hunger' partaking of the 'body' of the Mass, and of the 'apple that once was *the* apple', the fall of humankind from grace. Borodale's line 'the whole of time slows to a single spasm' reminded me of Yeats' 'For one throb of the artery, /While on that old grey stone I sat.../I knew that One is animate,/Mankind inanimate phantasy,' an unconscious echo perhaps of the Irish poet. Like McCaffery, Borodale likes the gritty word or phrase ('Bletted-by-heart', 'swarf') that carries physical conviction, but overall there is just too much blood and guts in this collection for my taste. A final point for future editions of the book: it is Penelope, not Persephone, who unpicks her loom each morning in the *Odyssey* (cf the poem 'Gratin', on page sixteen).

Helen Mort's *Division Street* comes highly praised by Carol Ann Duffy, but I just can't see it – in this particular group of poems anyway. I do know she was specially chosen as an *Agenda* Broadsheet poet and highlighted in *Agenda*'s pages a while back, so perhaps it is just here that I have a blip. There is a redolence of the poetry workshop about every poem in the collection, an idea or a concept (the Miners' Strike, Northern comedians, anorexia, spiders, Lakeland jogging, her dogs) worked to exhaustion. The rhythm is often limp, the ideas tired (and clichéd) and the 'diurnal grind' excessively emphasised. One or two poems I admired ('Division Street' and the translations from Tarkovsky) but the volume overall left me cold. A poetry of lists (see for example 'Carceri d'Invenzione') was long ago exhausted by Walt Whitman, and surely does not need reviving, although theoretically, given the epigraph from the writings of R L Stevenson, she does recognise the necessity for simultaneity and duplicity in art, but is unable to carry it off in practice in this instance. Heavyweight epigraphs are minefields for inexperienced writers. You have to be sure to tread carefully through them. Mort recognises the pressures of tradition ('you are lifted/by a finer thread, like all the living/anchored by the dead') but these pressures are very theoretical in this volume.

A far more accomplished book is Rebecca Goss's *Her Birth*, a lengthy sequence of poems recounting the short life of the poet's daughter, Ella, who suffered from a rare and incurable heart condition, and the joys and complexities that come with the birth of another child. Helen Dunmore has rightly said that 'The poems... unfold their story of love, loss and grief for a baby daughter with pared-down precision and scorching intensity,' and Bernard O'Donoghue has added 'But even such a powerful and moving narrative as this would not be effective without the beautifully crafted language in which the poems are expressed: clear, graceful, word-perfect'. The complexities of the emotion can be seen in the poem 'Another', describing the birth of her second child: 'Assure me I will not howl her name//during birth, that I will place/newborn fingers in my mouth,//taste only newness./Then I will consider another.' The narrative traces Ella's birth, the realization that something is wrong, the diagnosis, the post-natal care, the caring for a very sick child, the realization that her life will be short, the lack of a cure, the pain and division between the parents, jealousy towards other mothers, the medical paraphernalia, the child's death, the grief, the attempt to start life anew, the arrival of another baby, the guilt and joy of that event, and the recollection of earlier suffering and the pleasure of the new. The story throughout is told with tact and delicacy like an intense verse-novel, moving the reader to tears. To my mind *Her Birth* ranks with W D Snodgrass' *Heart's Needle* as a great poem of loss and grief, the grief at the suffering and death of Ella is harrowing throughout, and quotation can only curtail the overall effect. The sequence is structured in three sections: 'Echo', the first, considers the joy of Ella's birth, then the heart-breaking diagnosis, 'Mining' explores the feelings and daily traumas surrounding the child's illness and death, and 'Welcome' lastly serves as a coda to Ella and a salutation, reception, for the new child. The structure is musical in conception, resulting in a very moving experience. Style, form and matter merge in the book, so that the multiple associations establish links, every element reverberating like a chord, ideas becoming physical and not merely isolated abstractions, each possible connection teased out delicately. The book belies Yeats' belief that passive suffering (is there such a thing in any case?) is no fit subject for poetry. Out of personal grief fine work is forged. The bravery of the mother is evident on every page of this wonderful book.

Wendy Pratt writes of 'dark days' of loss, of climate change (an abiding theme, rightly enough, for young poets), car journeys, the sea's mercilessness, despair at the loss of a child (as in Goss' volume), all closely observed: 'the sun blanched and sick;/poached disparately in a white sky./A sea fret has fallen through/the bright morning, cutting the day/in two...' Kim Moore has written that 'these are subtle and necessary poems, mapping out the difficult business of moving on from trauma through a connection to the ocean and the creatures both real and mythical that inhabit it'. 'The sound of the sea wakes me/and I think, as always, of my girl/in the ground and how still/she must be...' The poems are living, vital, and well worth a read.

Sarah Sibley is aware of tradition 'as voices, long confined to cemeteries,/ reaching us like the light from a dead star', but also as something that can weigh you down, haunt you and scare you at the same time: 'Decades turning the same mattress/in this house of your forebears – /their ghosts stuck in the chimney flue,/forever bearing down on you.' There is a feeling of the centuries crowding you out everywhere. 'A local habitation' still has a name in Sarah Sibley's poetic world, as we listen to her praising the glories of living in a small Suffolk village in *The Withering Room*: 'she walked barefoot on the snow,/slept with every window open/inviting a coldness to match her own', charting the village's 'changeable weather', its humour, its domestic events:

Her first vacuum, a baggy lung in Scots weave
romping over carpets, spitting pennies and other heavy goods.
When its insides were shot,
she hoovered one carpet square at a time.
Then the Dyson was invented:
cyclonic, balding her fifty-year-old carpets –
airlifting them. Showcasing sedimentary layers
of toe nail, dead skin, hair.
Fascinated, she spent the whole week vacuuming
her mattresses, showing neighbours the contents
over the garden fence.

This poem reminded me of Jane Austen's Highbury (updated, in miniature), as did the fine title-poem 'The Withering Room'. I could imagine a modern Miss Bates nattering on for hours about her grand new hoover, and how everyone should rush out to buy one! It is refreshing to see some fine irony and satire in such a young voice. There are times these days humanity seems in too much of a mess for satire or irony to have any meaningful effect, but these qualities come to the fore in Sibley's verse. Paul Farley has written that these poems 'give evocative shape to a private vision,' but I disagree. The vision is a very public one, concentrating on the strengths and foibles of the poet's neighbours, breaking what the American poet Richard Eberhart calls 'the cosmos of aloneness'. This is a wonderful pamphlet, telling a short story in verse that is well worth reading. I think the poet deserves a full-length book, not just a slim pamphlet. There is dignity and strength in all of these poems.

Isabel Galleymore's *Dazzle Ship* demonstrates a fine sense of *poesis*, of making, showing wit and discipline at the service of an intellect not in the least bit dogmatic or assertive as other poets who take the environment as their subject matter can be at times, more concerned with the 'message' than the verse itself. There is nothing obtrusive, nothing egregious in these poems, no experimentation for its own captious sake. There is an inevitability, an integrity, to each of the poems that shows maturity at work. Every poem has an internal authority, a complexity of poetical structure, each lyric, as she writes, 'has folded itself so it can unfold... like the conch shell trumpet/ blown, but filling again/with its own sea-sound'. Galleymore's compressed metaphors work together to suggest the inter-connectedness of all living things, a working method best shown in 'Harvest', a poem which perhaps owes something to the Border Ballads:

After stripping the branches of berries
the robin held a handful of seeds
in her stomach: the robin carried a tree
– in fact she secretly sowed a whole forest –
a store of bows and arrows and shields.
   Years found the bird had planted a battle,
her tiny body had borne the new king.

Men looked up to the skies and blessed
or blamed the planets moving overhead.
A blackbird, meanwhile, started to pick
at the fruit the armies had left.

What I like about Galleymore's verse is the mature philosophy behind it, one secured in the necessity of identity, which after all is the quality most required of a distinctive poetic voice: 'two lovers grew so close they became/too fluently familiar/having lost what makes fire fire'. A person is an individual soul, as indeed is every word, for 'words that overlap', she writes, 'lose sense', and her poems strike a necessary balance between intimacy and distance that reason and sanity require of us, the necessity to get one's materials in order so that one can follow the history of a mind – 'My head upon a pillow/where your hand would rest./How much offered, how much withdrawn, by what my head already holds'. This is much less bitter than W H Auden's 'Lay your sleeping head, my love,/ Human on my faithless arm', and much more tender. There is a fine, delicate lyricism that I greatly admire in this poet. Galleymore explores the 'chemistry' of analogy and simile, finding likenesses in dissimilarities which Aristotle said was the hallmark of every true poet. There's nothing sentimental or fancy-fretted here. Galleymore finds 'The tone of voice, the choice of words,/the ambiguous intent behind/Each stone that forms the battlement' (from her poem 'A Castle or a Folly') and I look forward to reading more of her work.

Each young poet here has found their own voice (though some still have more ground to cover), a difficult achievement in a world plagued with distraction and noise. To find that voice requires intellectual attention and artistic concentration, and one can only admire any attempt in that direction. In Richard Eberhart's phrase, these poets speak the lyric that should live. Most of the poets have opted to write in free verse, the most difficult of forms to carry off (as Eliot memorably argued, 'no verse is free for those who wish to do a good job'). Such verse is *en courant,* and is thriving in the hands of these poets who all need encouragement as they continue to learn their craft.

Editor's note:
Readers might be interested to know that all the poets reviewed here, apart from Kate Miller and Sean Borodale, have appeared in *Agenda*'s online Broadsheets for young poets and artists, or in *Agenda*'s pages as specially chosen young Broadsheet poets, before any publication in pamphlets or collections.

Other promising collections received (no room to review them here) from Broadsheet poets are: David Briggs' *Raid Rider*, Emma Lee's *Ghosts in the Desert*, Isabel Bermudez's *Extranjeros*, Ben Smith's *Sky Burials*.

Eleanor Hooker

The Geography of Memory: Dublin as Metaphor

Jessica Traynor: *Liffey Swim* (Dedalus Press, 2014)

Liffey Swim, Jessica Traynor's debut collection, was published by the Dedalus Press in 2014. In 2015 it was one of four collections shortlisted for the prestigious Strong/Shine award for first best collection by an Irish poet.

The book is divided into three sections, naming three of Dublin's rivers, the Dodder, Liffey and Tolka. It is the Liffey that flows through the heart of the city.

In poems that are at once assured and disarming, and with more than an occasional nod to Joyce, Traynor chronicles a physical, emotional and historical landscape of Dublin.

'The Dead' is for me, the standout poem in the collection. Boldly taking its title and theme (the importance of the many dead in the lives of the living), from Joyce's famous story in *Dubliners*, Traynor takes ownership of the subject matter and upends it. In 'The Dead', Traynor sublimates anguish at her Grandmother's death through a description of the mischievous, noisy and crapulent dead, returning to claim the dying. The dead were...

> clamouring for space in the cramped kitchen,
> poring over her mismatched crockery,
> arranged not largest to smallest
> but according to some apocryphal code.

The terms, at which Traynor accepts her Grandmother's death, are utterly, utterly beautiful.

> In the small hours she called for them
> and, when her life escaped her,

> it shook out its legs like a newborn foal
> and found itself part of the herd.

Traynor takes Virginia Woolf's quote 'On or about December 1910, human character changed' as the epigraph to her poem 'Human Character'. This quote is widely accepted as Woolf signaling the arrival of Modernism in literature.

'Human Character' is a meditative poem that ponders on the mindset of Woolf the day she chose to wade into the river Ouse. In the first line of the poem, Traynor quotes from the last paragraph of Joyce's story *The Dead*, but admits Woolf 'would not approve of that', acknowledging Woolf's private, vociferous dislike of Joyce, (whose modernism, it is thought, influenced Woolf's writing style in *Mrs Dalloway)*.

Given Woolf's troubled mental history and the content of the two notes she left behind, the tenet for this poem seems more a fixing-in with the collection's themes, and therefore strikes a rare dissonant cord.

The South African poet Don Maclennan wrote 'A poem never drains/its ground of silence'. Traynor's poems have an exquisite subtlety that allows them to speak, and be silent, to accommodate the imagination of the reader. This is a skill that demands restraint, deftness and a lightness of touch, ever evident throughout this collection, for example in the poem 'Egrets in the Tolka'

> Above me, the happenstance
> Of hollow bone, dusty thermal,
> Becomes an aerial show
>
> by a bird that looks through me...

The place names in the poems in *Liffey Swim* ground them in the Dublin cityscape and give a magnificent sense of belonging. A theme of weaving, and unpicking the geography of memory features in many of the poems, and the theatrical subject matter of the poem 'Pearls at Blackfriars' reflects the poet's day job as Literary Manager at the Abbey Theatre in Dublin. *Liffey Swim* is an assured debut collection by a gifted Irish poet, of whom we continue to hear great things.

Translations/Versions

Laura Corraducci

i

fresh air in my locked rooms
each night you come closer to me
burning my desire to remain
this cleansing my feet in the mud
I feel like water under the microscope
the molecules fall from your lips
you move the curtain aside
and over the bridge the river flows
how can you fill every single nook
dilute your absence in a glass
quench all my thirst within a fire?

ii

I have built a beautiful boat to love
I picked up some wood in the forest
I didn't stop drawing your face
in the dust winding my legs
the thirst of sun wounded your lips
I put it into the pot over my head
I pushed the wind to not make you fall
and I spread petals of red flowers on the road
so you wouldn't hesitate to see the way
I perfumed my body in the ocean
I will leave my dress near the palm
I have built a beautiful boat to love
the sea has been waiting for us since ever
from this land we will sail with the moon

Note:
The first line of the above poem is the first verse of an African song the poet heard in
Cotonou, Benin.

iii

three inches of skin I sewed
on your waist as a tight belt
three stitches fixed on your hips
three crosses on your Golgotha of flesh
so come the wind
to untie me from your haunches
so come the fire
to burn me within a thunder
like a butterfly melt on the wall
today I will steal the scars to death

iv

you've never had white hair
they were just threads
fallen from your sweater
absently I picked them up in the car
on our Montefeltro hills
so now I understand that even pain
can choose his colours
to sicken our memories

v

you mix your voice with the fog tonight
close the windows let the show be for me
I see you with your hands in black and white
the contours of your lips always shaded
a ghost who is passing by
to put the soul in a body who rejects her
I'm cut off as a shoot from the vine
dry wood with no fruit for September
the sirens of ships are like an orchestra
and I see the lights behind the hill
if you prayed for a farewell
that wouldn't be so nice

Translated by the poet from her native Italian

147

Dome Bùlfaro

from Prima degli occhi (Before The Eyes Were)

Ictus no. 1 | Bone Structure Of A Family

beautiful to see you dying like this: / locks heavy with green figs
disrobed of the thirty years, / to see the agony of the breasts as they swell
inside the skin we will no longer be: / we shall die as parents, a family,
we shall fish a skeleton from the womb. / the navel wind-planted with
a seed, a seed that sparked a hearth / to which frost will show bitterness,
beautiful this forehead of ours as it cracks, / our eyes falling to pieces,
of a beauty without milk, a milk /without lips, lips already decreeing
no longer two: we've snatched an egg / from the nest, all night watching
with a candle the beak in the crack / in the crack the broken sparrow of our
couple with counted kisses, / our wild perfection
two peach blossom petals on the table, / that's the mutual threshold: a foetus
is but a flame inside our shadow, / had it stayed there, without speaking,
unresolved, its petals on the table, /had we stayed in the kitchen garden as shadows
of the foetus, going along with the nettles, / not thinking how much loss
spring carries in her breast, how many faces fade / into us & bleed from our hip
into stretched forward time, so it was / we recognized inside the bee forever
stretched out on the ground our own six / folded arms, beauty at rest.

collapsing like two wounded angels, / ass in the air drool on the pillow
night lamps all around / silently curved over the bed of the crime
warming us wrapped in ruffled sheets / the knife deep between our legs
fainted with pleasure in the sleep of time; /found like this we'd be pronounced
dead, not by the one who chose us, he knows / we sleep under a cover of butterflies
with red snow in our mouth – foetus / I'm too young to melt
into mother, to renounce my bark / of pomegranate split at the crotch –
have an abortion? what do you want? / to sleep in the palm of your hand
to be a backsurge of the universe / in the panting of a poplar flower,
in the bare stem that scratches us to understand / birdsong clearly.
you'll be your own last wild call before / being reborn, you'll forget
who what you have been before the eyes were; /in the shadow you'll believe us
to be your parents, we'll believe that / with you, and so, forgetfully,
will everyone, as detached from light we gravitate/to the colour of bones, of doubt,
attracted by what darkens us most; / one dies like this through a dripping

of forgetfulness.

one freezes like this / through some forgetfulness.
one dies / through forgetfulness.
torn to pieces by torpor

148

Ictus no. 3 | Breathing Pattern

times & vaults where & when the sea calls to us
& in one day returns us / to the earth as a wet cat,
a dragonfly or a lily: it's the inability / to breathe the heights of the abyss
offloads us back up to the surface, / uttering words like sacks
of spuds that tumble a few ramps down / running out of breath.
revolution begins in the breathing, / in the diaphragm lighting up beauty in
transience,

from this womb in which a tiny sunflower / seed teaches us freedom
from our own dying images / hastily pinned to the shoreline ...
– a snail does not resonate only / within the conclusions of its own shell –
a strawberry too, whether or not it prays, / will bend to the earth its slender stem.
the cosmos all that breathes calls out again, / fear not, people all know one another
except they don't know it, that's why they die / hungry: only a few know how to love,
it's all we've yet to learn / cages us here in condensation that won't
get going, in kisses strangled with lemons / not caring about infection,
we must learn to drown in no hurry / drown the keel before it is forsaken
each wave has a word in which to shipwreck / in which it slowly decomposes,
it's mud too liquid for / human hands to hold, we slowly drown
from the first day to the last – you who hypnotize me have / a lantern in your hands
when you stroke my

abdomen, when you open the pod for light to sketch / tender broad beans, a vision:
on the flat open sea

a cat sits like a king licking himself / on a floating trunk, the sea is a
perfect blue circle

each time the cats sets thinking / he falls into the water, thrashes around & comes
soaking back up, in

a few hours none will hear him meow. / a dragonfly hooked to the trunk and a lily
will wonder about the sense when they're too tired / the three of them will become
three white hairs –

the waves: a brief rush onto the sand then back to the sea
man: a brief name on the sand and then back to vital oblivion
if I the woman should by my fate / be first of us three to die, I hope I won't
be meowing for too long in my son's placenta, if I should be / the second of us three,
as a dragonfly & lily

I ask to be buried where the breath of the sea / breaks, of us three
should I be the last one to die, like the trunk I'll have seen / everyone die,
I'll recall all of my deaths

I'll have breathed everyone's death, before then / I hope I'll know how to drown
slowly slow in the placenta

of the word 'sea', there where everyone knows everyone / where everyone is
the waves: a brief rush onto the sand then back to the sea
man: a brief name on the sand and then back to vital oblivion

between vital breath & breath: transpiring the huge infection into salt

Ictus no. 4 | Cardiocirculatory

to the heart, before the whitewash, to the / heart before the anaemia
of poppies, have to bury unbury yourselves / take from the mallow don't know
how many infused leaves, before / the heartbeat reaches the endstop
and words come undone / alarmed like anthills on fire
to throw open over a whole lifetime / the book read on the face by gusts
in the heart, this dishevels the oval of the face: / those who are born solace sorrow,
those who die uproot it from chrysanthemums / believe me, one does not come
into the world
through the stopping of foetal / circulation, but through operating on the heart

a mute stain, from the boat / you can make out a mute stain growing
as it surfaces, it will ask / the world for breath it will ask
for the breast the arms but I will be mute / for three months mute, he alive in my
tomblike silence but mute, / as if I he were not, until three
months, anything but mutes, – *you never / know, often enough embryos wither back*
to spiders retreating / in the interspace – after three months
you're alive, the cord will connect us / our bloods must not mingle;
at the end of the third month / circulation won't be able to tell
good from evil, I'll not be able / to enter your lungs, those closest to us
will understand that I've been / someone else for three months: the one with
swollen belly, swelling / feet, the one whose mood swings
her outlook's been swung / & now she has bees in her bonnet
with her boss woman / giving me notice – the sack –
she says with resin in her mouth, / & flies chasing me into the house
as I weep I draw a furrow / with my face between me & the rusty flies
– sacked because pregnant – / anyone you tell will turn to rust.

It's not I who are pregnant with you / but infinity with itself, for three
months I too have been a foetus in / my foetus's womb, in myself
expecting the end, / from circulation to circulation
the blood of one's house / in the streets, in the partner as in others'

houses, in the blossoming heron; / the secret is here, in the breath of the heart
while we're close we change / we're watching each other change all the time
touch me for the last time; / I take you you unform while I'm next to you:
before the membrane covers / the eyes over, leave us half alive
half chronically dead / in the heart: alive with foetal
circulation still active post-partum, / connected to the world's cord like
parasites, believing the heart / will birth you between sorrow & joy
it will not be this me I am now, / you'll not be the mite you are now,
we'll be two newborns on the / relics of two other us, both inadequate
this is clotting in our hearts, / during each transhumance from day into
night, here the heart beats, where / everything is near quiet, my heart

our moving fragility / is not fragile in the heat

Translated from the Italian by Cristina Viti

From the Author's Note:
Before The Eyes Were is a meditative journey through and by means of poetry, deriving
from a deep personal change in consciousness, as experienced by the three protagonists
of the book: two young people on the verge of becoming parents, and the future child
who will determine the birth of a family – each going through their own joyful loss
as the self transforms and the borders between opposites such as life & death are
impossible to draw.

Henri Bauchau

Two poems from *Géologie* (1958)

i

To Philippe and Anne-Marie Jaccottet

Sometimes I wake with a taste of bark
in the mouth, a taste which comes from the rise of saps.
Perhaps I knew a great joy at the summit
and slept in the ceremony of branches
when they forged the union between the skies waters
and in the paternal trunk hirsute winter.
Perhaps in childhood or its vain pursuit
perhaps in the desertion of light
I heard that which spoke to me in a low voice:
hope no more, hold yourself firmly to silence.
So, nothing then, like a trout's jump at dawn
I'll leap into hope, a beautiful moment.
Perhaps having left the circle of the lamp
sleeper, did I touch the weft of night.
Perhaps I heard the one who guided me
after the tender maternal water, by the rivers
of clawing time, towards the place where one realises,
saying: Desire no more. To what use!
To be or to desire, that is the question demanded.
Stop finally this machine, if you want
to properly hear being and wed it to the deepest
marriages. So, on this well scrubbed surface
barren and with nothing than the beautiful nows of the earth
the forests will become the tree's will

The bird of May throws me a brief cry, as pure too
as foals' grass on the banks of innocent waters.
For the soul resides in the landscape of childhood
and may not leave there without growing old. What have I done?
Where is my peace? Where are the mornings of excellence?
Pious infant bearing his God in the joyfulness
like an aroma of hay, a cherry held to the ear?
The season moves and I form the tree, I stretch myself
to the summits of the soil and into the sky. Eros is there
in the blind root where I drank without seeing
the exquisite love of time that death renders savage.
Love and death knotted in the same tree, made
immortal by the acorn, the beautiful planter who plants
the life force at the heart of the real rose.
I who sound out the sap beneath wood, live
a schoolboy of the red thorn of new sense,
labourer of language and pruner who shapes
in the thickness of words the youth of language.

I give life if words are deeds
but their burning ambiguity tears into me.
I love what dwarves me, I burn, I am ashes
I consume my griefs, I lose my leaves
and this odour of death at my feet, that rots
these are my fallen fruits; others will perhaps go
to nourish in other places, people of another lineage.
Winter will come and I will make in rural landscapes
gestures of the blind with my horror-struck branches
to sense in the contraction of the cold
where warmth slept in the squirrel's death.

Translated from the French by Will Stone

Osip Mandelstam

A golden thread of honey hung from the mouth of the jar
Falling so sticky and slow, their host could speak out boldly
'So fate has driven us here, here to wretched Taurica,
Still there's plenty to keep us busy.' And she glanced over her shoulder.

All around they do service to Bacchus, go out and you won't see a soul –
Only watchmen here, and dogs, as if they walked the earth alone.
Like heavy barrels of wine, the days quietly roll
And the murmur of foreign voices echoes from distant homes.

After tea we took ourselves out to the garden, brown and wide,
Dark blinds on the windows lowered in modest gaze.
We walked the white colonnade the better to see all the vines
Where the hills lay asleep in the air's vitreous glaze.

I said then, vines, like an ancient battle, give yield
Where curly-headed riders fight in tangling coils
And this is the science of Hellas, in Taurica's stony fields
Here are golden acres of the noblest rust-red soil.

But in the white room silence – as real as a spinning wheel
And it smells of vinegar and paint, and wine, newly fetched.
Don't you remember the house, the Greek wife loved by all.
Not Helen, no, another, how long she sat and stitched?

Where are you, golden fleece, where have you gone?
How the heavy waves beat loudly for days and days
And when he left his ship the canvas sail was worn
Odysseus had returned, full of time and space.

Translated from the Russian by Sasha Dugdale

Pyotr Koshel

The door opens and father comes in:
– where's mother?
The door opens and mother comes in:
– where's father?

So they search and search for each other
While the blizzard whistles and howls
And the walls of the hut shudder.
My father Zhenya, and Vera my mother.

The door opens and father comes in:
– where's mother?
The door opens and mother comes in:
– where's father?

In this bitterest brittlest world
Alone and with no belief in beyond,
Wiping the angry untimely tears
I am listening to their questions.

The door opens and father comes in:
– where's mother?
The door opens and mother comes in:
– where's father?

Translated from the Russian by Sasha Dugdale

Louise Labé (1520?–1566)

Two sonnets

Sonnet 2

O beautiful brown eyes that turn from mine!
O scattered tears, o heated sighs
O darkness longed for all day – in vain
And dawn returns and light, and who knows why

O nagging desires, o pathetic groans
O squandered hours, o wasteful anxieties
O thousand deaths, a thousand strangleholds
O worst tortures you could wish upon me

O smile, o brow, hair, arms, hands and fingers
O plangent lute, viol and bow and singer –
So many torches to touch one woman's tinder ...

My one complaint: you come with such fire
Licking into such places, not least my heart
Yet onto you there flies not one hot spark.

Sonnet 3

Desire that pools and spreads. Hope – for what?
Aching sighs and tears of such long habit
That rivers inside me surge and rise
Founts and springs appearing in my eyes

Such stoniness, such cruel inhumanity
Makes celestial light glow warm with pity
Molten by primary passions and cooled, how
From this rock, my heart, could more woes grow?

Let Love try out his bow on me once more
Strike with sharper darts and stronger fire
Let him do his worst, till he's done undoing

For every part of me is so shot through
I'm unassailable – nowhere will he find
A fresh site, to make a fresh wound.

Note:
The Stoics named four primary passions: Distress, Fear, Lust, Delight

Translated from the French by Olivia McCannon

From *Evvres de Lovize Labé Lionnoize*. A Lyon par Jean de Tournes, avec Privilege du Roy. 1555. (Text as per *Oeuvres Complètes: Sonnets*, élégies, *"Débat de Folie et d'Amour", poésies*. Ed. François Rigolot. 2nd ed. Paris: Flammarion, 2004. Orig. pub. 1986.)

Lucretius

Fear and Greed

(On the Nature of the Universe 2.1-61)

it's sweet
behind your one-way glass
to watch onscreen the suicides, flung stones
the burning tyres, the barricades, the smoke:
not so much for the keen pleasure
of witnessing other people's self-destruction
but because you feel yourself
outside it all –
that's sweet.

sweet, too, when you see armies
massing on the map
below your secret vantage-point
more like a game of chess than men –

nothing sweeter than to look down
as from a lighthouse lantern room
buttressed by wisdom, and survey
the cowed and mutilated figures
refugees in search of Life – boat people
dragging their exhausted limbs ashore
gasping to come out on top
in mind or status or possessions.

pathetic human beings, needlessly blind
don't you know you're just clinging on
to the shadowlands of life?
and all the while your Self cries out to be let in
asking nothing more
than for the pain to stop
so the mind can revel in its freedom
to explore its happiness unburdened.

the body doesn't need much:
hardly anything – just enough
to take the pain away – but this small thing
lays out a feast before us.

the Self is closest
when you're lying in some park
grass tickling your cheek
the sky a mosaic in lapis lazuli
and quartzite for the tessellated candles
of the horse-chestnut up above
with some to spare for clover flowers below;
kids' voices trickling by, remote
like a river in the middle distance.

we don't die more painlessly on silk than polyester:
so, since all our bling and blood and power
can't keep death's hands from off our flesh,
how can they help our inner Selves?

– unless you think that when you see
our soldiers playing war
dealing death at one remove
to those whose distance makes them small
these troops can chase away your fear
that there might just be a God
and that He might be just;
or make the fear of death release
its shackles from your mind.

don't you see?
the things we value most
make us look the biggest fools:
the fears we share
the cares that dog our steps
don't retreat in the face of smart weaponry
but work the room like PR reps
without respect for panoply –
and only Reason routs our fears
when life is bowed in shadows.
and just like children fear

what lurks behind the shadows, dark to sight,
so in daylight adults are afraid
of things less real
than the nighttime fears
and fantasies of children.

the sun's weapons, brittle lances of light
can't scatter the mind's black horrors:
only if we peel open nature and look in.

Sensations

(On the Nature of the Universe 2.398-443)

atoms stroke us, grab or shake us,
perforate or wound us, according to their shape
wherever bodies offer them a breach.

honey and milk roll with pleasure on the tongue
while bitter things – absinthe, espresso –
shrink the lips and pull the mouth into a grimace.
sweet things massage our tongues
with smoothly rounded atoms, one by one;
when substances seem sour and bitter, these
assault the tastebuds in hooked entourage
and storm our bodies in battalions.

All things that rouse our senses with their touch
are pleasant or unpleasing, according to the build
and shape of their components. rough's opposed to smooth:
tooth-jarring saws don't play on our ears
with elements as smooth as those
that steam up from some honeyed tango,
when the guitarist strokes his strings awake
like a sleeping woman;

mass graves' smouldering effluent
clogs our recoiling nostrils with offscourings
quite unlike the scents that drift from roses
thrown onstage at some ballet,

or when Tibetan incense brings
the Buddha's body rising from the shrine.

you needn't think that those good wholesome colours
your eyes can't get enough of
are made of like components to the ones
that puncture your eyeball and force the juices
out, or military shades – depressive greys and khakis
which guarantee compliance just by looking –
their atoms scratch your eyes like tiny burrs
you can't get rid of.
another kind of particle's not altogether smooth
or completely formed of countless little hooks
stuck one into the other; these are more like
the pointed shapes in a kaleidoscope:
cornered forms which arouse but don't maim
the senses: think citric acid, or the pleasing bitter taste
of raw opium straight from the plant.
these substances have teeth of varying gauge
which prick the senses in their different ways
their touch upon our bodies tells us what they are.

touch is almost like a god-given thing
touch reaches through
the straightjacket of membrane
which keeps each self shut in
its own unique asylum
touch gives us the illusion of contact with the world
or makes us listen to our bodies
when they're wounded from inside
or when sex starts its chain reaction,
waves of pleasure lapping deep within
our bodies from outside; or when some psychosis
tangles our senses around one another
and brings complete emotional collapse:
self-harm's the physical corollary of that effect.

so atoms with their different forms
play in different keys upon our senses.

Translated from the Latin by Emma Gee

NOTES FOR BROADSHEET POETS

Sarah Howe interviewed by Patricia McCarthy

Sarah Howe, 32, is a British poet, academic and editor. Her first book of poems, *Loop of Jade* (Chatto & Windus, 2015), won The Sunday Times Young Writer of the Year Award and the T.S. Eliot Prize. Born in Hong Kong to an English father and Chinese mother, she moved to England as a child. Her pamphlet, *A Certain Chinese Encyclopedia* (Tall-lighthouse, 2009), won an Eric Gregory Award. Her poems have appeared in journals including *Poetry Review*, *Poetry London*, *The Guardian*, *The Financial Times*, *Ploughshares* and *Poetry*, as well as anthologies such as *Ten: The New Wave* and four editions of *The Best British Poetry*. She is the founding editor of *Prac Crit*, an online journal of poetry and criticism. Formerly based at Gonville and Caius College, Cambridge, she is a fellow at Harvard University's Radcliffe Institute in 2015-16.

P McC: Sarah, welcome to *Agenda*'s New Generation Poets' issue. You are very much a young 'New Generation Poet' who has had a meteoric rise to fame with your first collection, *Loop of Jade*, published by the major publishing house, Chatto and Windus and reviewed here on pages   .. You have already won many prizes, and awards for this and have also given several interviews. Therefore, here, I am going to try to ask you questions that I hope, in the main, haven't been asked of you.

SH: Thank you Patricia, it's a pleasure to be asked.

P McC: How are you coping with all the attention and publicity?

SH: I'll confess it hasn't all been easy. Maybe I'll be able to talk about this one day, but right now my instinct is towards a self-protective quiet. I've been holding in mind this thought of Randal Jarrell's: 'Tomorrow morning some poet may, like Byron, wake up to find himself famous – for having written a novel, for having killed his wife; it will not be for having written a poem.' At the same time, I'm pleased and honoured that the book seems to be finding new readers as a result of the awards. The way poetry is often covered in the press suggests a sort of arm's-length incomprehension, even a secret rage, that a medium which asks time and effort of its readers should continue to exist. On the other hand, I've met some wonderful journalists recently who really care and think hard about how to change that superficial narrative. And the way *Loop of Jade* has been embraced by readers – even by people who say they wouldn't normally pick up a book of poems – is something that continues to surprise and humble me.

I think I'm learning to make sense of prize culture as essentially an outward-facing exercise. For better or worse, it's a system designed to show off a very limited tranche – too much would overwhelm a press-release – cut from the bustling sphere of activity which is the writing and publishing of poems. Those of us who breathe in that world, by contrast, know how much extraordinary work is being done all the time which doesn't receive accolades or press, but is no less important because of it. I have to say, my own fascinations as a reader often lean in the direction of such under-the-radar work.

P McC: It seems to be typical of today that poets have to be PR people for themselves, even when much lesser known than you. Is there a contradiction in you, for example, between the shy, private, even hermetic person that writes the poetry and the public media peripatetic person that you have to become?

SH: I don't know that you have to become a public media peripatetic person exactly (though I do love the tongue-twisteryness of that phrase). I really don't feel all that 'known' myself, though I would be glad for the work to be known, which is a different thing. I agree it's important to guard one's inner reserves of silence. Where else are the poems going to come from? The natural impulse to privacy, I'm just beginning to understand, is particularly fraught for poets. So much of what makes lyric compelling is to do with its seeming to open a window onto a vivid inner life. There's an intimacy and a vulnerability involved, or the necessary impression of those things. People will assume the experiences conjured in the poems map directly onto the poet's life. I find the game of 'autobiographical' bait-and-switch played by the title poem of Frances Leviston's *Disinformation* both acute and instructive in this respect.

As for poets being their own PR people, I find social media interesting on that front. I've never felt native on Twitter, finding the idea of it quite frightening at times. But I do delight in following many poets, including some whose poems feel inevitably and excitingly bound up with the medium. What those writers do isn't self-promotion, but something altogether more interesting: it might better be described as curating fragments of a personhood. You'd be foolish to leap on those snippets as candid self-revelation, but they still have that frisson.

P McC: Your poetry is particularly topical at the moment (although of course a universal, timeless issue) concerned, as it is, with refugees, immigration, displacement, with being, as Derek Walcott puts it, 'divided in the vein' since you are half English and half Chinese. Do you feel that your own background has actually given you your poetry? For example you so articulately say in the poem, 'Crossing from Guangdong', 'My heart is bounded by a scallop shell'…

SH: I'm quite resistant to readings of that kind, since I fear they push in the direction of treating poems as a symptom of their maker's biographical origins, ultimately reducible to or explainable by them. I'm doubly wary when questions of race or culture are thrown into the mix, since I'd want instinctively to disavow that sort of determinism. At the same time, I know this wariness must sound perverse on my part, since *Loop of Jade* does circle obsessively around these very preoccupations. Undoubtedly there is a compulsion being worked out in the book, but I hope it's a knowing rather than a naive one.

I'm so glad you quote that wonderful line of Walcott's, whose work has been a huge influence on my thinking. If I remember right, 'A Far Cry from Africa' is one of the early poems that consider his place in the world as the descendant of two white and two black grandparents:

> I who am poisoned with the blood of both,
> Where shall I turn, divided to the vein?
> I who have cursed
> The drunken officer of British rule, how choose
> Between this Africa and the English tongue I love?

What chimes with me is how that idea, 'divided to the vein', quietly reveals itself as a paradox. Its literal impossibility underlines the slipperiness of 'race': how to separate out the 'white' capillaries from the 'black' ones? And yet our history is overshadowed by exactly such fragile projects of racial taxonomy and classification. Their influence is at once pervasive and barely visible today, like the onetime laws of hypodescent that mean we would never refer to Barack Obama as America's white president. My own poem, 'Others,' touches on these historical currents: 'Some words die out while others survive. *Crossbreed. Half-caste. Quadroon.*' I wasn't aware of it until the late stages of putting together the manuscript, but there is a pun running through *Loop of Jade* on the idea of the *crossbreed* (a word that sometimes turned up in my hearing during my later childhood in England) and the *crossing* of geographical boundaries, especially water – as in that poem you refer to, 'Crossing from Guangdong.'

The Chinese term for people like me, 混血 (*hùnxuě*), has its own tangled skein of past associations, meaning literally 'mixed blood,' but with just a hint of 'muddled' or 'confused blood.' In early twentieth-century colonial Hong Kong people like me were a taboo, vulnerable and even fetishized subgroup: an unpleasant reminder of what ensued when the Empire's implicit racial hierarchies were transgressed. They often survived by plumping for one side of their heritage (usually the Chinese, since the British were still more inhospitable) and doing everything they could to outwardly 'pass' in that identity. *Loop of Jade,* especially its central Borges sequence, is my way of exploring the extent to which identity is imaginary, fluid, historically determined, politically contested, up-for-grabs. That's a long way of saying we might need to flip round your interesting formula. Maybe it's less that my background has given me my poetry, than that I'm interested in how poetry might give me – or any of us – our backgrounds.

P McC: Your collection is such a tour de force, with wonderfully vivid, startlingly accurate images, often like those in Chinese paintings. Interesting that until you started to write poetry in earnest aged twenty one that, from childhood on, you painted mostly. Do you think that it was your new outsider's eyes in a Hong Kong that you did not know that helped you to conjure these images so freshly?

SH: Thank you, that's very kind. As you say, the fantasy of becoming a painter was one I'd kept up throughout my late teens and never really escaped. After university I spent a year doing nothing but paint, trying to get together enough work for an art school portfolio. I also travelled to mainland China for the first time, producing a lot of photographs and sketches, but no writing as yet. I even spent a while learning how to paint with Chinese brush and rice paper, though in pursuit of a Western rather than more traditional optic. I made many ink paintings of the same disappearing landscape around the Three Gorges Dam that features in my poem 'Yangtze,' though I'm glad none of them survive. At the end of that spell, I made a decision that felt like a huge turning-point: to give up on painting and embark instead on postgraduate work in English literature. I set myself on the path to a PhD, but also felt a sort of grief at letting go of that other part of my self. The poems started to come shortly after that choice, as a compensation I think: the same enquiry pursued by other means.

Interesting that you should ask about Hong Kong and 'image,' since a sort of surreally heightened sensory dimension was one of the dominant notes in my adult re-encounters with the place. The thing that bowls me over every time I travel there – and I remember this most vividly from my first trip back aged sixteen – is the smell that greets me off the plane. Maybe I should say scent rather than smell, since I mean an inherently pleasant thing. I find its precise quality hard to describe, hemmed about by clichés of Hong Kong as 'Fragrant Harbour'. Yet it wasn't the smell's exoticism that hit me so much as its uncanny familiarity: the smell of my early childhood, and yet one entirely forgotten until I was delivered back into its presence, in that unaccountable, Proustian way. There's a line in one of my poems, 'Islands,' that gets some way towards it, albeit in the voice of a character much like my mother: 'sea-drizzle, diesel, damp, black hair.'

P McC: Perhaps most poets are outsiders of some sort. As you say, 'The poet is always in a foreign country'. Are there any other ways than being 'divided in the vein' in which you would consider yourself an outsider?

SH: It does resonate with me, that saying. It belongs to the French-Jewish-Egyptian poet Edmond Jabès, who knew something about borders and allegiances. Part of me worries that the notion of 'poet as outsider' might be an unhelpfully romantic obfuscation. But speaking for myself, I guess I was always the sort of child who would minutely watch the pavement as she walked; the sort of child who, after years of following the same route, would still have no clue which direction the school bus would take next on account of having such an intense imaginative life. During my first seven years in Hong Kong I learned one way of being in the world, then had to intuit a new set of social codes in the playground in Watford. If anything, I tried to learn how to mimic the behaviour of others so perfectly that I wouldn't be marked as an outsider.

P McC: This leads on to your treatment of 'memory'. Because your mother's own biographical details are incomplete, you have, in a sense, had the liberty to make up bits of her past, using your own experiences to patch up her life. Yet, do you think most of us use memory like this, as part-invention, maybe subconsciously, even when we have all the facts and details?

SH: That's an excellent description of how I feel memory works all the time. I tried to think about this phenomenon in the first of a series of essays I wrote for the *Best American Poetry* blog: the process by which I would write poems drawing on my early memories of life in Hong Kong, then go back to the island on a sort of fact-checking mission only to realise that certain, vivid details couldn't possibly be right. It became important to me to preserve those hiccups and fillers as an authentic element of recollection, a way of acknowledging the unreliability involved in accessing the past.

Those glitches – as small perhaps as that style of decorations hung at one of the local temples in a given year – might only be apparent to me, or to a native Hong-Konger, but they felt like an important component in the 'truth' of my relationship with the place. Poems like 'Crossing from Guangdong' explore precisely this overlaying of – and discrepancy between – the place I might visit in reality and the Hong Kong of my mind. As you say, so much of my orphaned mother's background is mysterious and most likely undiscoverable. What flooded in to fill that vacant gap in my family tree wasn't so much imaginative reconstruction as an engagement with Chinese myth and history at a macro-scale.

P McC: How far do you consider your studying of English Literature at University, followed by a Ph D in Renaissance Literature, and your career as a university teacher and literary critic stymied or held you back from your own creative writing? After all, you say you did not write poetry until you were twenty one. Or did your academic studies enhance your poetry?

SH: I'm not sure I would say that one stymied the other, since until I was twenty-one I didn't really have anything invested in the idea of writing poems, so there was no frustration there. One thing I did notice early on was that I found the business of editing poems, and of commenting on the poems of others, quite challenging at first. My training as a literary critic had been about developing an account of what a given combination of words on the page was doing, rather than seeing a way through to the best form they could take. I don't know about my academic research enhancing the poems. I tried for a long time to keep those parts of my life separate from each other. Thinking back, I can see how much my poetry was shaped not by the academic world I moved in, but by the lively London poetry scene that became a refuge during my PhD: all the friendships, writing groups, the crucial ties of artistic influence and mutual support I found there. At the same time, I acknowledge there is a more 'academic' strain in my work too, sometimes serious, sometimes half-parodic. For example, there's a scholarly, hyper-referential tone that I was conscious of letting some of the later poems inhabit, playfully licensed by their connection to the book's Borges epigraph, and channelling some of his fondness for linguistic curios, intellectual world-building and blind-alleys of thought. To leave out such a strain altogether, I felt, wouldn't offer a true portrait of how my mind works or the cultures that formed it, though I do realise that pushes me further from the poetic mainstream.

Tugging against that aspect of my work is how important it is for me, when sitting down to write, to find ways of ducking the rule of the conscious intelligence. I need to get into something like a meditative state: among my habitual routes to that place, one is to jot down lists of disconnected words temporarily severed from sense. The painter Cy Twombly used to go through phases of drawing with his wrong hand in an attempt to bypass his own skill and training. For me the most productive writerly state of mind is one where I feel, at least for a time, I've delegated all thought and responsibility to the hand moving the pen.

P McC: Yes, I understand that kind of lightness: when you almost mustn't think lest what you write turns out too heavy. I can detect in your collection much play on words or metaphysical conceits reminiscent of Donne, and sometimes even a Hopkins' joining of words for full texture. Along with your literary and classical allusions, there is a mix, even, of surreal images, and use of familiar traditional nursery rhymes. Were all these used consciously, or dredged up unconsciously from your psyche?

SH: It crept up on me slowly, the realisation that several of my poems seem to hinge on something quite like a metaphysical 'conceit.' It wasn't until I'd already finished poems like 'Sucking Pigs' that I understood this, having always thought there was no trace of writers like Donne in my reflexes, despite spending so much time immersed in their world. That poem turns on a neat and somewhat amusing reversal that occurred to me in the lead-up to our wedding. One of the central Chinese wedding traditions involves the gift of a roasted piglet as an emblem of the bride-to-be's chastity, while in my husband's culture, Judaism, the pig represents the absolute opposite of purity. The poem structures itself around the poles of that cross-cultural irony, which in practice work a little like a joke – though not necessarily one that would make you laugh out loud.

I like your account of the raw materials of poems as relics dredged up from the depths of the psyche. I think that was very much the case with the Chinese myths I've mentioned, which crept into the poems cumulatively and by different routes. For example, the legend of *Chang'e* – the woman-turned-goddess who accidentally swallows her husband's pill of immortality and is punished by floating off into the sky to live forever on the moon – is one I heard retold every year at Mid-Autumn Festival, like all Chinese children. For reasons I didn't understand at the time of writing, that story seemed an essential ingredient in the poem called 'Islands' about my mother's childhood. Some time after finishing the poem, I was talking to my mum about researching different versions of the myth, and she told me something I'd entirely forgotten. Apparently every time I heard that story as a small girl it would make me cry. I suddenly remembered why: *Chang'e*, lonely on the moon, blurred always in my childish mind into the figure of my own mother, growing up an orphan separated from her real family, utterly alone. Writing the poem reactivated that old association, yet without it impinging on my conscious mind.

P McC: Isn't there an equal danger in academics believing they can automatically be gifted poets, and Creative Writing graduates thinking they, too, can all get published to high acclaim?

SH: I don't know about the first scenario – though I suspect many of the experimental poets who find shelter in the academy would take issue with the ideological underpinnings to a phrase like 'gifted poets'. But there is certainly a tinge of sadness in the latter idea. I'm reminded of a brave and clear-eyed blog post Clare Pollard wrote a while back comparing – I might be misremembering – the dynamics of Creative Writing degrees to those of Ponzi schemes. That's obviously the most pessimistic view, and one I think Clare didn't wholly subscribe to herself. By and large I suspect most poets, including graduates of such programmes, would continue to do what they need to do as writers regardless of worldly recognition. We can all learn from that.

P McC: Do you think undergraduate Creative Writing degrees are a good thing? And the postgraduate ones? Would you like to have done these? And would they have benefitted your poetry? Or do you think it best to find your own voice in isolation?

SH: I'm not terribly knowledgeable about such degrees myself, but anecdotally I can say that a huge percentage of my peers, the new and upcoming poets I most admire, have been through that type of formal training in Creative Writing. Whether such degrees add value to talent that was already there isn't my place to judge, but I really don't see any signs of the deadening, homogenising influence that people sometimes attribute to such programmes. From what I've seen I suspect they do a deal of good. For a long time, I was part of the more informal equivalent – a trusted group of poets banding together round a table to ask for and offer insights on new work – and that was a huge part of forming me as a writer. Sometimes you simply can't understand how a line will come across (or not) to a reader who isn't you, which is where other eyes become so valuable. Eventually you learn how to trust your own instincts, but internalizing those querying voices is an important step on the way.

P McC: I notice you did enrol, while at Harvard, in a semester's workshop with Jorie Graham. Was this worthwhile for you and, if so, why?

SH: It was essential: the scales fell from my eyes. I casually enrolled for a ten or twelve week course with Graham as a new graduate student in America. I'm not sure why, given I'd never heard of her before that point, or ever written more than a handful of poems. What followed was the most revelatory training in how to 'close read' poetry, its minute rhythms and mechanics on the page, but from a viewpoint I'd never really glimpsed till then – the 'inside' perspective of the working practitioner. What we read together were overwhelmingly the masters of the American tradition – Stevens, Williams, Dickinson, Bishop – and further on to their inheritors in the present. Having never really encountered it till then, I fell in love with American poetry in a way that continues to shape my tastes and habits of thought.

P McC: I have observed how you fuse, like Jorie Graham, image and idea. In fact, you very successfully combine images with abstract philosophy, which is a difficult thing to do, especially as there is a danger, I would think, of leaving the world of images which poetry requires to make it alive, when delving into philosophy and intellectualising.

SH: Actually I've never had much truck with analytic philosophy myself – I'm much too blurry and unstructured a thinker to survive for more than a dip in such waters. I'm often fond of Wittgenstein, to pick one body of philosophical work I've made more of an effort to engage with. But it's very much a poet's fondness, seizing on felicitous local metaphors and ideas like truffles. So, for example, one of my recent poems riffs on the wonderful image of a jigsaw puzzle that crops up at one point in the *Philosophical Investigations* – 'sky is always the hardest part' – in the course of Wittgenstein's speculations about language and other minds. Or looking back to *Loop of Jade*, my little poem 'Earthward' could be described as a quarrel with Plato, not that I think that gloss particularly helps bring it into focus. I imagined that poem quietly taking up the mantle of one of my absolute favourites by Graham, 'Reading Plato,' from her early book, *Erosion* – the one about the fishing flies. But at the end of the day, I'm with Sir Philip Sidney in preferring the sensuous realm of the poet to the abstract one of philosophy. Sidney's argument is that poetry can in fact do both, offering 'to the powers of the mind an image of that whereof the philosopher bestoweth but a wordish description, which doth neither strike, pierce, nor possess the sight of the soul.' I don't think I would seek to defend poetry today in quite his terms, as an instrument of moral education, yet his *Defence of Poesy* has long been a touchstone for me.

P McC: I don't know if you are familiar with Gjertrud Schnackenberg's *Heavenly Questions* (which I reviewed in the Keenings issue of *Agenda*, Vol 46 No 2), but your work reminds me slightly of hers: full of erudition and music, though some readers would find both you and her quite inaccessible at times. What is your view of accessibility in poetry?

SH: I don't know Schnackenberg's work, but I'll have to seek it out on the basis of what you say here and below. On the more general question of accessibility, I don't think 'difficult' would be a particularly helpful label to apply to my work, even though it's the term we usually reach for to describe the end of the stylistic spectrum with the sorts of ambitions you describe: it makes reading sound like a chore, which is not what I'm after. I believe the poetry ecosystem needs to support a range of different types of work if it is to stay healthy. My own taste as a reader is broad – I find things to delight in Duffy and Hill, Agbabi and Prynne – and I'm conscious of trying to forge a style that might learn things from both sides of those longstanding stylistic and ideological oppositions, incoherent as that might seem to some. The aesthetic pluralism sometimes identified among my generation of poets has been called 'post-division' or 'hybrid.' Given how involved *Loop of Jade* is with the idea of racial or cultural hybridity, its range of styles bears a conceptual, even a political, force for me.

I value poetry that jolts you out of the usual run of language-habit, that invites you to dwell in mysteries – mysteries which over many visits might or might not resolve. On the subject of what it means to 'get' a poem, I love an essay called 'My Impasses: On Not Being Able to Read Poetry' by the American poet Maureen McLane, from her genre-bending essay collection, *My Poets*. McLane writes with delightful candour – and a refreshing lack of ego – about her student-days' panic and confusion in the face of poems she had no idea how to read. 'Many of the poets and poems now important to me,' she writes, 'were completely and maddeningly elusive when I first encountered them'.

I am fascinated by that threshold where one hovers, not getting it yet wanting to get it. Where a tentative desire contends with frustration. Where frustration may be converted into desire, and desire into some provisional illumination. As a poet, as a student, as a critic, as a teacher, as a citizen, I have found this vale of unknowing yet wanting-to-know to be a fruitful vale, a dwelling place worth sharing, pondering.

Not all of the poems in *Loop of Jade* work in the same way, or invite the same kinds of attention. Some I conceived as working more like abstract paintings, or even Buddhist *koans*, which walk through nonsense into another sort of 'unknowing'. This is where you'll see most clearly the mark that poets like Ashbery or Stevens have left on my work. What I was aiming for with such poems was to sidestep, or at least hold at bay, the conceptual intellect with its drive to interpret and decode, opening up other sorts of felt experience as a result.

There are certainly poems in *Loop of Jade* that approach a state of complexity I feel is true to my experience of the world. For what it's worth, I suspect we encounter more intractable instances of moral and linguistic complexity in life every day; it would be wrong to hive off poetry into some separate plane of experience. At the same time, I hope there are enough episodes of plainspoken simplicity, of sensual immediacy, in *Loop of Jade* to reflect what it's like when the world crystallises to a sudden clarity. The relationship between those two qualities, simplicity and complexity, is important to me. They might inhabit the same poem, or even the same phrase, but their alternation at a larger scale was a guiding principle as I put together the collection. That architecture was key. I thought of it as creating a reading experience that would feel almost like shifting between different levels of focus. I wanted to write a book that would offer up certain pleasures on a first reading, but then shift and deepen on later encounters.

As for 'accessible' or 'inaccessible,' I often feel there's an uncomfortable snobbery at work in the way the media deploys such terms when discussing poetry. I think you can see this dynamic in something a journalist said to me in person recently, along the lines of 'I have a First in English from Christchurch, Oxford and I find your poems mostly baffling, so what chance does anyone else have?' I find that patronising, disingenuous concern for some sort of darkly alluded-to uneducated mass of people especially riling. I myself am endlessly grateful for the education I received: an enduring privilege and pleasure that I know remains a remote possibility for too many. But I've also always been conscious of coming from people who had nothing like that kind of educational advantage – and that this was something important to remember. I'm uncomfortable with a view of the arts that slips too easily from categorising poems ('This is an easy poem', 'This is an obscure poem') to categorising people: dividing up an imagined readership into a group who will appreciate and those who won't, on the basis of assumptions about education or class or race or whatever.

I was the first person in my family to go to university. My mum grew up in a degree of poverty that *Loop of Jade* barely dares to imagine, and yet she – my dad too, in a different way – is the most extraordinary autodidact: an unsystematic, chaotic, occasionally hilarious thinker whom I fiercely admire. She attributes her first steps in English to a university student who spent a summer doing volunteer work at her school in Macau, long enough to teach the children the rudiments of phonetic reading. Landing a job as a typist in Hong Kong, she taught herself English to a level of mastery that goes beyond many university-level linguists – not that such a career option would ever have been on her horizon. Her bedside table has *Harry Potter* on it one week and Herodotus on it the next, because that's the way her natural curiosity works: it doesn't occur to her to limit it. For as long as I remember she has hoarded books to an almost pathological extent, a tendency she once attributed to the fact she didn't have access to any when growing up. In fact, the only volume I know she definitely owned in the early part of her life still sits on the shelf at home: an anthology of the Tang dynasty poets.

This is why I've been so delighted by the warmth of response to *Loop of Jade*, coming from an audience wider than I imagined possible. If you don't constantly tell people poetry is too difficult and not for them, maybe they won't think it's something they have to shy away from. Whenever I felt it would offer a helpful hand to the reader – a piece of information or a translation I thought it might be useful to know – I added a note at the back of the book. Yet it seems to me the question of accessibility can no longer work quite the same way in an age when so many of the traditional trappings of poetic difficulty, whether of vocabulary or reference, can be illuminated in thirty seconds on Google. That's not to say there's no such thing as a dense or intimidating poem any more. I remember what it felt like to be put on the spot at school with the dreaded 'What does that line mean?' (Exam boards don't like dwelling in mysteries.) But I care about creating conditions that might allow such work to be enjoyed beyond a narrow sphere.

P McC: Interestingly, Gjertrud's collection, like yours involves an odyssey through different cultures and religions, mythologies, sciences, physics; mixes old and new worlds, and also highlights, among myriad themes, the theme of writing that she links to the ancient banished Chinese poet, Qu Yuan. Ancient Chinese poets are important sources of reference and energy in your collection too, as well as names and even Chinese characters – and the poems involving these divert from the more prosaic autobiographical sections. Is the inclusion of these an attempt at universality, at invoking a whole cosmos to heal the split 'in the vein' and to 'sing beyond sense'?

SH: That's very kind, and the theme of ancient Chinese poets in exile – fittingly, the emperor would always banish them to the far West for their transgressions – has been a big part of my thinking too. I can see how it might feel like *Loop of Jade* is reaching for a sort of 'universality' at moments like the ones you describe. But for my part, I feel that sort of aspiration to universal (cross-cultural, trans-historical) truths is mostly undercut in the poems, albeit sometimes quite slyly. For example, the poem called 'Drawn with a very fine camelhair brush' might look at first like a fable about the awesome perfection of Chinese characters and their ability to capture reality, but it's one with a sting in its tail. The poem begins with the speculations and projections of European thinkers, including the early Jesuit Missionaries, who from the seventeenth-century started to wonder if the ideographic basis of Chinese might make it a candidate for the true 'universal language,' believed lost since Eden and Babel. Readers familiar with Ezra Pound's edited version of Ernest Fenollosa's essay, 'The Chinese Written Character as a Medium for Poetry,' will know that this fantasy of Chinese's 'visual' immediacy persisted well into the twentieth century, despite being founded on a basic misprision about how the writing system actually works. I don't want to give away the punch-line, but the scholar-poet navigating the river of linguistic meaning in that particular poem ends up losing his boat.

P McC: Presumably Pound (who actually founded *Agenda* with William Cookson in 1959) is a major influence and even a mentor for you. Can you comment on this? I think he would preside very proudly over *Loop of Jade*.

SH: Yes, Pound is definitely one of the tutelary figures who sit behind *Loop of Jade*, via both *Cathay* and the *Cantos*. The Chinese characters you mentioned, which hover in the right-hand margin of several of my poems, allude to the visual presentation of the *Cantos*, preoccupied as Pound was with Chinese etymology. I first became fascinated by Pound as the inventor of Imagism, though I subsequently came to see how right Eliot was when he called him 'the inventor of Chinese poetry for our time.' I don't think any Chinese poet writing in English even today can get round that legacy without confronting it in some way. In practical terms, I found *Cathay*'s intuitively brilliant but sometimes linguistically ill-founded moves as a 'translation' from the Chinese oddly enabling, not least as a way of navigating what sort of cultural space I might inhabit as a half-Chinese person who grew up not speaking Chinese: is it possible to recuperate a Chinoiserie-like 'inauthenticity' – that being the way I sometimes think of myself and my Western reference-points – at the same time as critiquing it? Those were the sorts of questions Pound as poet-translator opened up for me, as well as demonstrating the power and flexibility of the poetic 'persona,' which became such a vital strategy in *Loop of Jade*. It's funny, but I don't think of my poems as straightforwardly autobiographical at all, but more like a series of masks I might let slip to varying degrees. Finally, Pound's troubling politics, particularly of race, became an explicit theme in a poem like 'Stray Dogs.' There the historical Pound, awaiting trial for treason in his DTC cage near Pisa, becomes a figure for thinking through the limits of free speech on the one hand, and the limits of empathy on the other.

P McC: Eliot, too, seems to be there somewhere, particularly in the *Four Quartets'* theme of journeys and never arriving.

SH: I hadn't thought of that, how interesting... It's certainly true that after first falling in love with *Prufrock* in my late teens after a chance encounter in the school library, it was *Four Quartets* I next pulled off the shelf. I photocopied several pages from it – I forget which ones – which sat blue-tacked above my desk throughout my A-levels. I recently stumbled again across Eliot's 'Chinese jar' in 'Burnt Norton' for the first time in ages...

> Only by the form, the pattern,
> Can words or music reach
> The stillness, as a Chinese jar still
> Moves perpetually in its stillness.

...and realised that it must lie behind the poem of mine I talked about just now, 'Drawn with a very fine camelhair brush,' where the slender wings of dragonflies are 'a marriage of stillness and furious motion.'

P McC: Are there any other major influences on your work?

SH: I usually end up answering this question with reference to poets, but it occurs to me that other genres and art forms are at least as influential on the texture of my work. For example, among the many visual artists who are important to me, the work of Chinese conceptual artists like Song Dong and Xu Bing has helped shape the way my poems deal with understanding across languages, silence, erasure and historical trauma. Fiction, too, often provokes new poems for me, sometimes more so than reading other poets. I was first drawn to the novels of David Mitchell because of their frequent Far Eastern settings, and resulting exploration of cross-cultural communication and sympathy. But other features of his work, including the books' intricate, interlocking architectures, their underlying metaphorical currents, their exploration of causality on a dizzying historical scale, became if anything even more influential on the poems that went into *Loop of Jade*.

P McC: I read somewhere that your next book will be a long poem responding to the Umbrella Movement in Hong Kong that enshrines the principle of 'One Country, Two Systems' and runs out thirty years from 1997. I think you said you would be looking at this from human, legal and political angles. Does this mean there will be less autobiography here, and less of your own persona in the next lot of poems?

SH: *Two Systems*, as it's called, ventures into more conceptual territory than I've explored in print before, though I've always been interested in that sort of avant-garde, procedure-driven work. It's an erasure poem that, as you say, takes as its source text the 'Basic Law' or mini-constitution of Hong Kong. The poem is made up of whatever words remain behind when I've finished blanking out the majority of each page with the Photoshop eraser tool. That formal conceit has become an anarchic, unpredictable, but potent way for me to explore the idea of disappearing words, disappearing freedoms, disappearing booksellers. I no longer think *Two Systems* would make much sense as a book, or at least not one published in the UK: it might work better as a piece installed in a gallery or (somehow) on the street in Hong Kong, or as a freely distributed chapbook. I'm due to visit Hong Kong in November 2016 for the literary festival there, and it will be the first time I've read in the place of my birth. My mother is much too worried about my going – she thinks I'm going to be bundled into the back of a van – despite my frequent attempts to reassure her of the many reasons why that won't happen, one which is that no one in authority knows or cares about my existence. If that sounds uncomfortably flippant, it's the humour of grim desperation. The more I work on this new poem, the more I find myself grappling with what it means to write in solidarity with the people of my native place, in sympathy with their fears and disappointments, yet without having to undergo the same risks or political consequences. Then again, perhaps those who can speak have a responsibility to do so.

P McC: Seamus Heaney warned about the dangers of confronting politics head on in poems; unless you take politics from a subtle angle, he said, the poem runs the danger of turning into a political slogan. What do you think about this?

SH: The political poems in *Loop of Jade* work, I fancy, a little like that cognitive science experiment where the subject is so intent on counting the number of times the ball passes between players that he or she doesn't see the man in the gorilla suit walking clean across the basketball court.

P McC: Do you always write in sequences i.e. get on a kind of roll and make a whole fabric of individual poems which all relate to each other in diverse ways? You must write random poems sometimes which come out of the blue. What happens to these?

SH: In fact, I think I mostly write random, miscellaneous poems whose place in the order of my obsessions becomes apparent only later. The Borges sequence in *Loop of Jade* was an exception to my usual working habits, but one that was thrilling to pursue as a result. A good two-thirds of those poems emerged thick and fast over the course of one month – then the final remaining pieces took several years to write and slot into place. It was as if the nearer I got to the end, the more remote a prospect it became, like the 'impossible heap' of sand in Beckett's *Endgame*.

P McC: Do you feel nervous about your new collection: that it might not match up to *Loop of Jade*'s resounding success? Again, referring to Heaney, I know he considered he had been awarded the Laureateship too early, and that, in a way, it limited him as a poet since normal ordinary life then became a rarity and he had to go round being 'a poet'.

SH: If I ever want to write or publish another poem, I think I'm going to have to try to block out anxieties of that sort. It might feel hard right now, but I suspect the sheer pleasure and necessity of writing will carry me once more. Plus, I don't think I quite have Heaney's problems of name-and face-recognition to contend with!

P McC: Have you had acting lessons, or studied Drama, as you read your poems beautifully, even speak them by heart? This is rare in a poet, for you have a real professional presence in your delivery on stage and in recordings for the BBC radios 3 and 4.

SH: Performance is increasingly important to me, partly spurred by seeing incredible readers of the calibre of Kei Miller, Kayo Chingonyi, Inua Ellams, Warsan Shire, all of whom have in different ways changed my understanding of what poetry can do. I've always been terrible at acting, but the memorising and speaking aloud of poems was a constant presence in my childhood from quite young. For a few years from about eleven my mum enrolled me in something called 'speech and drama lessons,' taught by a woman I adored, whose original Irish accent I was somehow aware had been transformed by her time at RADA into the cut-glass RP I learned to imitate. We spent half-an-hour together every week or two in term-time, as she offered directions in how best to perform, with understanding and feeling, the poem I'd learnt by heart that week – everything from James Fenton's 'Tiananmen,' which I still have mostly by heart, to long speeches from Shakespeare. I don't often have occasion to recall those sessions, but doing so now, I'm startled to see a sort of blueprint for my future life –

as both poet and Renaissance scholar – laid out in miniature across those half-hour lessons. It was only as I got a bit older that I started to realise how it was basically just me and children from nearby South Asian families that attended them. I can now see how it was partly a project of immigrant assimilation-anxiety and social aspiration, driven on some level by those parents' need for their children not to be marked out by accent as their generation had been. Funnily enough, I discovered while chatting one day to my co-editor at *Prac Crit*, Vidyan Ravinthiran, that he went through much the same experience during his childhood in Leeds: he wrote a brilliant poem about it in his first collection, *Grun-tu-molani*.

P McC: Now to the obvious question: what advice would you give to young poets? Would you tell them to chant them to themselves, as you do, when writing them, and also to pen them in the small silent hours?

SH: Chanting is helpful, as is going through a distinct drafting stage where you think about tweaking the poem for nothing but sound. I'm sadly getting too old for my small-hours writing these days – all-nighters now tend to wipe me out for forty eight hours after – so I'm not sure I can recommend that strategy to anyone.

P McC: Sadly for *Agenda*, your new poems are 'all under wraps'. Does this mean you send out every poem you write and judge them all to be of an equal standard? Can you even write to order?

SH: I like how 'top-secret' that sounds! The truth is that beyond the erasure sequence I talked about before, I'm not writing many poems at the moment, being too distracted by prose side-lines. It feels like a long time since I've had a big sheaf of poems ready to sort into piles and send off to magazines. On the question of quality control, I've always found that quite hard to judge myself, so I rely on the help of trusted friends and the wonderful editors I've worked with in recent years. I enjoy writing to order – the last poem I wrote for a commission involved spending a couple of months reading about nothing but theoretical physics. That was a happy time.

P McC: Well, thank you so very much for this enlightening interview and let us hope that that jade bracelet, that 'loop of jade', so hauntingly given to you by your mother's adoptive mother, will continue to be a protective talisman. Let us wait for it, when touched by you, to put you in communication with the past and past generations as well as with the present and future for your next keenly awaited book, and all that follows thereafter.

Biographies

Born in Belfast in 1993, **Jacob Eoin Agee** attended St Michael's Primary School (1997-2004) and Royal Belfast Academic Institution (2004-2011). He has recently completed a four-year joint honours BA in Jewish and Islamic Civilizations, with Classics. He divides his time between Belfast, Dublin, and Korčula in Croatia. His poetry has appeared in *Poetry Ireland Review* (Issue 111, edited by John F. Deane) and the TCD literary journal *Icarus* (three times).

Henri Bauchau was born in Mechelen, Belgium on 22 January 1913. He became a trial lawyer in Brussels in 1936 and was a member of the Belgian Resistance in the Ardennes during WWII. In 1946, he moved to Paris. He was a friend of Albert Camus, André Gide, Jacques Lacan, and Jacques Derrida. An original European voice, Bauchau wrote prodigiously and travelled extensively, publishing a series of highly successful novels and latterly became a kind of Belgian literary icon, partly due to his venerable age. Bauchau died in Paris, France on 21 September 2012, aged 99. There is now a highly dedicated Henry Bauchau Foundation at the French language University of Louvain-la-Neuve in Belgium.

Elizabeth Barton, 42, read English at Christ's College, Cambridge, after which she moved countries and had a family. She has worked as an English teacher and written freelance articles published in *The Times* and *The Catholic Herald*. She lives in Surrey and is a member of Mole Valley Poets.

Charlie Baylis lives in Spain. He reviews poetry for *Stride*. His creative writing has featured in a number of magazines and e-journals, including *Stride, Ink Sweat and Tears, the Cadaverine, the Delinquent*, and Agave. Charlie has been nominated for the Pushcart Prize, the Forward Prize and for Queen´s Ferry Press´s Best Small Fictions. He has made the shortlist for the Bridport prize. He was (very briefly) a flash fiction editor for *Litro*. *Elizabeth*, his debut pamphlet is out now from Agave Press in the US.

Zoë Brigley-Thompson is a native of Wales but is now Visiting Assistant Professor in English at the Ohio State University. She has two poetry collections *The Secret* (2007) and *Conquest* (2012), both of which were UK Poetry Book Society Recommendations. She edited *Feminism, Literature and Rape Narratives* (2010). Among prizes conferred are an Eric Gregory Award, a Welsh Academy Bursary, the English Fellows' Poetry Prize, and *The Secret* was listed for the Dylan Thomas Prize. She has published poems, stories and articles in publications like *The Manhattan Review, PN Review, Calyx, Poetry Ireland, Poetry Wales, Women's Studies Quarterly, Poetry Salzburg,* and *The Times* (HE Supplement).

Dome Bùlfaro was born in Liguria in 1971. He is a poet, performer, visual artist and publisher. He has published several collections of poetry and read his work internationally (Edinburgh 2009, Melbourne 2012, Rio de Janeiro 2014). His pamphlet *Ossa* and the book *Ossacarne* have been translated into English respectively by Christopher Arigo (Interim 2006) and Cristina Viti (*Bonesflesh*, Le Voci della Luna 2012).

Will Burns, 35, was born in London and raised in Buckinghamshire. He didn't finish his English degree, choosing instead to start an ill-fated band with his brother. He has worked in factories, cleaning windows, painting houses and the best record shop on earth. He likes sports and ornithology and is Poet-In-Residence at *Caught By The River*. His poems have been published in *Structo* Magazine, *Ambit, Illustrated Ape* and the *Independent Online*. He was named as one of the 4 Faber & Faber New Poets for 2014 with his pamphlet, *Faber New Poets 10*, published in October 2014.

Peter Carpenter's new chapbook, *Peace Camp*, is published by Maquette Press. Previous collections include *Just Like That* (Smith/Doorstop), *The Black-Out Book* (Arc), *Catch* (Shoestring) and *After the Gold Rush* (Nine Arches). His poems have appeared in many literary journals and magazines including the *TLS, Poetry Review, Poetry Ireland Review, Stand, The Rialto, the Independent* and *The Independent on Sunday*. He is a co-director and editor of Worple Press.

Caroline Clark's first collection is *Saying Yes in Russian* (*Agenda* Editions, 2012). Poems and essays have since appeared in *Agenda, Snow, Tears in the Fence and Painted, spoken*. She translated the title essay in a book of work by Olga Sedakova, *In Praise of Poetry* (Open Letter Books, 2014), which was awarded a Heldt prize for best translation.

Paul Connolly's poetry has appeared in *The Warwick Review, The Reader, The Cannon's Mouth* and *The Dawntreader*. He was shortlisted for the 2015 Bridport Prize and won third prize in the 2015 Magna Carta Poetry Competition (judged by George Szirtes).

D. V. Cooke (David Vincent Cooke) was born in Cheshire and graduated in English from London University. He worked for a number of years for The Poetry Library in London and has published in numerous poetry magazines including: *Acumen, Babel, Envoi, Frogmore Papers, Orbis, Outposts, Poetry Wales, Stand, Swansea Review, Tandem* and *Agenda*.

Laura Corraducci was born in Italy, in Pesaro, on the Adriatic coast where she lives. She is an English and Special Needs teacher. In 2007 she published her first collection of poems, *Lux Renova* (Ed. Del Leone, Venice). In 2012 she won an important literary prize dedicated to female poetry: La donna si racconta. She has organized several poetry readings and a festival, vaghe stelle dell'orsa, dedicated to contemporary Italian and foreign poetry. She translated into Italian *Saying yes in Russian* (*Agenda* Editions) by the English poet Caroline Clark. Her poems have been translated into Spanish, English, Romanian, Dutch and Portuguese and are included in many poetry anthologies. In April 2015 she published her second collection of poems, *Il Canto di Cecilia e altre poesie* (Raffaelli editore).

Martyn Crucefix's recent original collections include *Hurt* (Enitharmon, 2010), *The Time We Turned* (Shearsman, 2014), *A Hatfield* Mass (Worple Press, 2014). He has translated Rilke's *Duino Elegies* (Enitharmon, 2006) – shortlisted for the 2007 Popescu Prize for European Poetry Translation – and Rilke's *Sonnets to Orpheus* (Enitharmon, 2012). *Daodejing – a new version in English* will be published in 2016. For more visit www.martyncrucefix.com

Tony Curtis is emeritus Professor of Poetry at the University of South Wales where he introduced Creative Writing and ran the Masters degree for two decades. He is currently Poet in Residence for the National Trust's Dyffryn Gardens in the Vale of Glamorgan. He took his talk 'My Life with Dylan Thomas' to the USA in September. His biog and publications are on www.tonycurtispoet@btinternet.com

John F. Deane was born in Achill Island 1943. He founded *Poetry Ireland* and *The Poetry Ireland Review*, 1979; published several collections of poetry and some fiction; won the O'Shaughnessy Award for Irish Poetry, the Marten Toonder Award for Literature, Golden Key Award from Serbia, Laudomia Bonanni Prize from L'Aquila, Italy. Shortlisted for both the T.S.Eliot prize and The Irish Times Poetry Now Award, he won residencies in Bavaria, Monaco and Paris. He is a member of Aosdána . His recent poetry collections: *Eye of the Hare* (Carcanet 2011). *Snow falling on Chestnut Hill: New & Selected Poems* was published by Carcanet in October 2012. His latest fiction , a novel, *Where No Storms Come,* was published by Blackstaff in 2010. A new collection of poems, *Semibreve,* was published by Carcanet in 2015 and a 'faith memoir', *Give Dust a Tongue*, was published by Columba, also in 2015 .

A poet and artist, **Karen Dennison**'s poems have been published in magazines such as *The Interpreter's House* and *South Bank Poetry* and in several anthologies including *From the City to the Saltings* (Essex Poetry Festival Anthology 2013). Karen's collection *Counting Rain* was published by Indigo Dreams in 2011. She is editor, designer and publisher of the pamphlets *Book of Sand* and *Blueshift* and her digital images/photos appear on the cover and inside Abegail Morley's pamphlet *The Memory of Water* (Indigo Dreams, 2015).

Sasha Dugdale is a poet and translator and the current editor of *Modern Poetry in Translation*.

Charlotte Eichler is 33 years old and lives in West Yorkshire. Her poetry has appeared in magazines including *Agenda* (*Broadsheet* 22), *The Rialto* and *Ink, Sweat and Tears*. She is a freelance book editor and assistant editor of the *International Medieval Bibliography* at the University of Leeds.

Tessa Foley is a 37-year-old writer and an administrator at the University of Portsmouth where she formerly gained her Master's degree in Creative Writing. In 2013, she won the Live Canon International Poetry Competition judged by Glyn Maxwell under whose tutelage she attended a poetry class in London last year. She has since been published in magazines such as *Antiphon* and *Star & Crescent* and was listed as a finalist in the *Poetry Rivals* competition. She is currently working on a novel about alcoholism, studying for a qualification in counselling and has recently become a member of Mensa. She originally comes from Flitwick, a tiny town in Bedfordshire.

Isabel Galleymore's debut pamphlet, *Dazzle Ship*, was published by Worple Press in 2014. Her work has featured in *Poetry Review*, *Poetry London*, *Ambit* and *Agenda Broadsheets*, and was commissioned by the Bristol Festival of Ideas. She is currently the Charles Causley Poet-in-Residence.

Emma Gee grew up in rural Australia and studied in Sydney and Cambridge. She has worked as a lecturer in Classics at the University of Exeter, the University of Sydney, and in St Andrews. Her interests include ancient astronomy and philosophy, the ancient afterlife, Renaissance Latin poetry, and psychoanalysis. She has just completed a book called *Mapping the Afterlife* which combines ancient philosophy and literature with music and psychology. Her *Lucretius* translations arose from a desire to make this astonishing text accessible. In 2015 extracts were published in *Tellus* no.6.

Kevin Graham lives and works in Dublin. Born in 1981, he has a BSc in Applied Computational Linguistics. His poems have appeared in various journals such as *Acumen, Magma, Stand, The Shop,* as well as the Templar anthology *Peloton.* In 2012 he was selected for the *Poetry Ireland* Introductions Series and in 2014 he was nominated for a Hennessey New Irish Writing Award.

Eleanor Hooker's first collection of poems *The Shadow Owner's Companion* (Dedalus Press) was shortlisted for the Strong/Shine Award for best first Irish collection 2012. Her second collection, *A Tug of Blue is* forthcoming from the Dedalus Press in 2016. Eleanor is Programme Curator for the Dromineer Literary Festival. She is helm and Press Officer for Lough Derg RNLI Lifeboat. For more details visit: www.eleanorhooker.com

Matt Howard is 37 lives in Norwich, where he works for the RSPB. Matt is also a steering group member of *New Networks for Nature*, an eco-organisation that asserts the central importance of landscape and nature in our cultural life. His debut pamphlet, *The Organ Box*, was published by Eyewear in December 2014. He was part of last year's Aldeburgh 8 at the Aldeburgh Poetry Festival.

Lucy Ingrams (49) has had poems in *THE SHOp, Ink, Sweat and Tears, Magma* and *Poetry Ireland* among other publications. She is studying on the MPhil Creative Writing programme at the University of South Wales under Philip Gross.

Valerie Jack's first full length collection, *Educational*, was published by tall-lighthouse in 2009. Hugo Williams has written of her work: 'Valerie Jack's pared-down hyper-realist vocabulary brings the world into high definition. Her poems are like arrows to the mark, we feel their impact.' Valerie's poems have appeared in the *TLS, PN Review, Magma, The Spectator,* and *The London Magazine*. Her play, *Fireworks,* was produced at the Etcetera Theatre, Camden in 2010. Recent poems have been inspired by life aboard her narrow boat.

Tess Jolly has had poems published in a wide variety of magazines. She has been commended in the Four Counties Poetry Competition, the Barnet Arts Competition and twice in the *Mslexia* Women's Poetry Competition. Last year she came joint second in the Stanza Poetry Competition and won the Hamish Canham Prize. A pamphlet is due from Eyewear Publishing this year.

Pyotr Koshel is a Russian-language poet, writer and editor originally from Belorus.

Anna Lewis was born in 1984. Her first full-length poetry collection, *Other Harbours*, was published by Parthian in 2012, and her pamphlet *The Blue Cell* is forthcoming from Rack Press. She has twice been *Agenda's* chosen young Broadsheet poet.

Twice shortlisted for the T.S. Eliot Prize, for *The World Before Snow* (Carcanet) in 2015 and *The Blood Choir* (Seren) in 2006, **Tim Liardet** has produced ten collections of poetry to date. He has also been longlisted for the Whitbread Poetry Prize, and has received several Poetry Book Society Recommendations, a Poetry Book Society Pamphlet Choice, an Arts Council England Writer's Award, a Society of Authors Award, a Hawthornden fellowship, two Pushcart nominations, and various other awards. *Arcimboldo's Bulldog: New and Selected Poems* is due from Carcanet. He is currently a Poetry Book Society selector and Professor of Poetry at Bath Spa University, England.

Louise Labé was a Renaissance woman. She lived in Lyon, the cultural heart of France at that time, a city with strong Italian connections. The daughter of a wealthy rope maker, she reportedly jousted, fenced, spoke several languages, played the lute and wrote poetry, including the sequence of 24 sonnets to which these two belong. In this sequence, she turns the tables on the Petrarchan tradition of the hard-hearted mistress, distant and cold, whose absence is a pretext for poetry, by writing verse in an assertive female voice, verse with a performative function, which actively seeks to make the lover present, to bring him to life (or at least his senses).

Lucretius: We construct a lie for ourselves. The world is not as we want it to be: tame and predictable. What we think we see is a mere perceptual skin stretched over the chaotic motions of unseen particles, whose more-or-less random motions in the Void give the world a surface semblance of order. In 55 BC, Lucretius sought to prove this, to an audience more accustomed to interpret the world through notions of divine order. He argues for the maverick element in the universe. Primary Particles (what we'd call atoms) exercise a capricious hegemony. The gods, while they exist, take a laissez-faire attitude to the world. They have reached the state to which we aspire, *ataraxia*, 'unconcern'. Lucretius' mentor was Epicurus (341-270 BCE), the originator of 'Epicurean' philosophy. But Lucretius' technique is his own. He speaks now as much as then – challenges us, makes us hoot with laughter, provokes indignation, shame, anxiety, and finally peace.

Originally from Perthshire, **Ailie MacDonald** completed her undergraduate degree in English and Creative Writing at Warwick University before going on to Aberdeen to study for her MLitt in Comparative Literature, during which she specialised in Hugh MacDiarmid's later work. She is 27 and lives in Sussex.

Antony Mair lives in Hastings and has just completed a Creative Writing MA at the University of Lancaster. He has been previously published in *Agenda* and has also had poems accepted for publication in *Acumen, The Interpreter's House, Poetry Salzburg Review, Ink Sweat and Tears* and *The Lake*.

Osip Mandelstam (1891-1938) was one of the most brilliant of an intensely brilliant group of poets in Russia in the first decades of the twentieth century. He was repressed by Stalin and died in transit to a labour camp.

Gary Matthewman performs internationally as a classical song pianist. He appears regularly at Wigmore Hall in London, and recent engagements overseas include Carnegie Hall in New York, the Musikverein in Vienna, Philharmonie in Paris and Bolshoi Theatre in Moscow. Past and future recital partners include Dame Kiri Te Kanawa, Sir Thomas Allen, John Mark Ainsley, Sumi Jo and Mark Padmore. He has made numerous recordings and live broadcasts for BBC Radio 3. This is his first published poem.

Richie McCaffery (28) lives in Stirling, Scotland and has recently completed a PhD on the Scottish Poets of World War Two, at the University of Glasgow. He has published articles and academic work in *The Dark Horse, Scottish Literary Review* and *Etudes ecossaises*. He is also the editor of *Finishing the Picture: The Collected Poems of Ian Abbot* published Kennedy & Boyd in June 2015. His collections are: *Spinning Plates* (HappenStance Press, 2012), *Ballast Flint* (2013) and *Cairn* (Nine Arches Press, 2014).

Olivia McCannon's poetry collection *Exactly My Own Length* (Carcanet/Oxford Poets, 2011) was shortlisted for the Seamus Heaney Centre Prize and won the 2012 Fenton Aldeburgh First Collection Prize. She lived for nine years in France and her translations include Balzac's *Old Man Goriot* (Penguin Classics, 2011), contemporary poetry and drama. She co-judged the Popescu European Poetry Translation Prize in 2015.

Bernadette McCarthy is a 31-year-old archaeologist living in West Cork, Ireland. Her poems have appeared in *The Linnet's Wings, Causeway/Cabhsair, The Lake,* and *Crannóg*. She edits the journal *Brain of Forgetting*.

Gill McEvoy: publications in print: *Rise* (Cinnamon press, 2013); *The First Telling* (Happenstance Press, 2014) which won the 2015 Michael Marks award. Gill runs regular and occasional poetry events in Chester. She is a Hawthornden Fellow.

Andrew McMillan was born in South Yorkshire in 1988; his debut collection *physical* was the first ever poetry collection to win *The Guardian* First Book Award. The collection also won the Fenton Aldeburgh First Collection Prize, and was shortlisted for the Costa Poetry Award and the Forward Prize for Best First Collection. It was a Poetry Book Society Recommendation for Autumn 2015. In 2014 he received a substantial Northern Writers' Award. He currently lectures in Creative Writing at Liverpool John Moores University and lives in Manchester.

W S Milne is a regular contributor to *Agenda*. He has recently completed a translation of the *Iliad* into Scots and a play on the life of the Scottish poet Robert Fergusson. He is currently working on an essay on *The Divine Comedy*.

Jessica Mookherjee is a poet with Indian heritage, brought up in Wales and lived most of her adult life in London. Now located in Kent, she has had poems published by *Ink, Sweat and Tears, Prole*, the *Journal, Antiphon* and *Gold Dust*.

Abegail Morley's new collection, *The Skin Diary,* is published by Nine Arches Press (2016). Her debut collection, *How to Pour Madness into a Teacup* (Cinnamon) was shortlisted for the Forward Prize Best First Collection. *Snow Child* and an ekphrastic collection *Eva and George: Sketches in Pen and Brush* are published by Pindrop Press. Her website is The Poetry Shed: www.abegailmorleywordpress.com

Stephen Noon – 27, Philosophy graduate & Theology postgraduate.

Luke Palmer is a 31-year-old Teacher of English from rural Wiltshire. He has recently become a father for the first time which has led to a greater appreciation in his writing of the majesty of the everyday. His poems have previously appeared in *Orbis* and *Agenda* and he continues to work towards a first collection.

Ben Parker was born in Worcester in 1982. In 2012 his debut pamphlet, *The Escape Artists*, was published by tall-lighthouse, and in 2013 it was shortlisted for the Michael Marks Award. His second pamphlet, *From the Porcelain*, was published by the Museum of Royal Worcester in 2015.

Sarah Parker is 32. She achieved a BA in English Language and Literature at St. Hugh's College, University of Oxford and an MA in Modern Literature and Culture, 1850-Present Day at the University of York. She currently works in publishing.

Georgina Pett-Ridge, 21, has just finished studying English Literature at the University of Reading, England. She aims to continue writing, and hopes in the future she will have more to put in her biographies.

Rachel Plummer, 31, grew up in Cambridgeshire. She studied Nuclear Astrophysics at university before moving to Edinburgh to establish an animal shelter. Her poems have won a Troubadour Prize, come second in the Penfro Poetry Competition and were highly commended in the Poetry on the Lake Competition two years running, as well as being commended and shortlisted for various other prizes. She has two young children.

Joseph Rennie (32) was born in Leek, a small town in the Staffordshire Moorlands. He achieved an MA in Creative Writing from Keele University. His work is shaped by his experience of growing up as a child of a struggling single parent labelled as schizophrenic. His poetry is an odyssey through pain, fear and heartache to love and acceptance, heavily influenced by the Beats.

Carol Rumens's latest collection is *De Chirico's Threads* (Seren, 2010). A new collection, *Animal People*, will appear from the same press in 2016. A Fellow of the Royal Society of Literature, she has published short stories, a novel (*Plato Park*, Chatto, 1988), a trio of poetry lectures (*Self into Song,* Bloodaxe, 2007) and worked on occasional translations of Russian poetry with her late partner, Yuri Drobyshev. She teaches Creative Writing at Bangor University, Gwynedd, and contributes a popular weekly blog,'Poem of the Week' to *The Guardian Books Online*.

Omar Sabbagh's poetry and prose (critical and creative) have appeared in such venues as: *Poetry Review, PN Review, Poetry Ireland Review, The Reader, POEM, Kenyon Review, Wasafiri, The Wolf, Banipal,* and elsewhere. His poetry collections include: *My Only Ever Oedipal Complaint* and *The Square Root of Beirut* (Cinnamon Press, 2010/12). A fourth collection, *To The Middle Of Love* is forthcoming with Cinnamon in late 2016. His Beirut novella, *Via Negativa: A Parable of Exile,* was published by Liquorice Fish Books in October 2015. He teaches at the American University in Dubai (AUD). www.omarsabbagh.me

Sarah Sibley was born in Suffolk in 1985. She currently lives in North Norfolk and works as a freelance copy editor. Her work previously featured in *Agenda 'Exiles'* and *Agenda* Broadsheets 25 and 15, and elsewhere has been published in *Iota, Orbis, Ink, Sweat & Tears, The Delinquent* and *Obsessed with Pipework*. Her first pamphlet *The Withering Room* is available from Green Bottle Press.

James Simpson is a Jerwood/Arvon writing fellow and won second prize in the Thomas Hardy Society's James Gibson Memorial Poetry Competition. He has collaborated with the book artist Carolyn Trant on *Hunting the Wren* (Parvenu Press) and *The Untenanted Room* (*Agenda* Editions). Their most recent work together, the artists book *The Rhyme of the Reddleman's Daughter,* is available as a limited edition from Parvenu Press.

Henry St Leger, 21, is a young poet, playwright, arts journalist and English Literature graduate. He had his modern stage adaptation of Ovid's *Pyramus and Thisbe* showcased at Brainchild Festival and was published in this year's issue of *The Mays* (XXIII) with a poem on *Grand Theft Auto*. His work has also appeared in *Ladybeard* (Body Issue) and on *playhouse64, thisspace,* and *YPN*. He writes on sexism, anxiety disorders, video games, and making art in the age of advertising.

Will Stone is a poet, essayist and literary translator. His first poetry collection *Glaciation* (Salt, 2007), won the international Glen Dimplex Award for poetry in 2008. The sequel *Drawing in Ash*, was published to critical acclaim in May 2011 (Salt). Shearsman Books have recently reissued these collections in new editions and will publish his third collection *The Sleepwalkers* in March 2016. His translations published by Arc, Menard and Hesperus include works by Verhaeren, Rodenbach, Trakl, Rilke, Nerval and Roth. Pushkin Press published his first English translation of Zweig's *Montaigne* in August 2015 and Zweig's *Messages from a lost world* will appear early in 2016.

Siân Thomas lives in East Sussex. Her work has appeared in various publications, including *Agenda, Poetry Wales, Swamp, The Daily Telegraph, The Rialto* and the anthologies *London Rivers* and *The Needlewriters Companion*. Her pamphlet *Ovid's Echo* is published by Paekakariki Press. She holds a Masters degree in Creative Writing from the University of Sussex and is Poet in Residence for Ashdown Forest.

Jessica Traynor is a thirty-one year old poet from Dublin. Her first collection, *Liffey Swim* (Dedalus Press, 2014), was shortlisted for the Strong/Shine Award. Poems have recently appeared in *Hallelujah for Fifty Foot Women* (Bloodaxe, 2015) *Poetry Ireland Review, One* (Jacar Press), *The Stony Thursday Book, The Irish Times* and *The Stinging Fly*. She is under commission by the Arts Council (IRL) to write a poem as part of the Easter Rising centenary celebrations, and was a runner-up in the 2015 Troubadour International Poetry Prize. She works as Literary Manager of the Abbey Theatre, Dublin.

Katelyn VerSprill, 24, is a poet, researcher, and messy cook who resides in Edinburgh, Scotland. Originally from New Jersey, she moved to the UK in 2014 to pursue her Masters degree at Lancaster University and is currently a PhD candidate at the same institution. Her poetry has appeared in *Killing the Angel* and helped her become the 2014-2015 Fulbright-Lancaster University Postgraduate Scholar. She has studied under the direction of poets Mark Doty, Eoghan Walls, and Paul Farley.

Cristina Viti's translation of Mariapia Veladiano's first novel, *A Life Apart* (MacLehose Press, 2013) was runner-up to the 2015 John Florio Prize. Other work includes *Stigmata*, a collection by major Albanian poet Gëzim Hajdari (Shearsman, 2016) and the first full English translation of Elsa Morante's *Il mondo salvato dai ragazzini* (*The World Saved By Kids*, Seagull Books, 2016).

Nicola Warwick was born in Kent and grew up in Suffolk. She has a Diploma in Creative Writing from the University of East Anglia and has had poems in several magazines and competition anthologies and was included in the *Agenda* online supplement to the *Opera* issues. Her first collection, *Groundings*, was published by Cinnamon Press in 2014.

Heather Wells' poems have appeared in several publications including: *The London Magazine, Agenda* and *Poetry Salzburg Review*. Her debut collection *Maiden Voyage* was published in 2014.

Patrick Widdess was born in Cambridge in 1979. He currently resides in Newport, South Wales where he works as a copy editor. He has reached the national finals of the Hammer and Tongue poetry slam twice and his poetry has appeared in publications including *The Guardian, Orbis, Ink, Sweat and Tears* and *Cake*. He runs the poetry blog and podcast *Headstand*.

Mark Wormald is Fellow and Director of Studies in English at Pembroke College, Cambridge. Educated at Oxford, he won the Newdigate Prize for poetry in 1988 and an E.C. Gregory award in 1995. *Stills and Reflections* was published by the Sycamore Press in 1989; poems have since appeared in various books and magazines. He has edited *The Pickwick Papers* for Penguin and has published on George Eliot, Hopkins and contemporary fiction and poetry; he was editor of *Oxford Poetry* magazine from 1988-1992. Several recent essays on Ted Hughes have appeared; he co-edited (with Neil Roberts and Terry Gifford) *Ted Hughes: from Cambridge to Collected* (2013), and is the editor of the *Ted Hughes Society Journal*. *The Catch: Fishing for Ted Hughes* will be published by Little Toller Books in 2017.